THE DEFENSE
TRANSPORTATION
SYSTEM

THE DEFENSE TRANSPORTATION SYSTEM

Competitor or Complement to the Private Sector?
Clinton H. Whitehurst, Jr.

American Enterprise Institute for Public Policy Research
Washington, D.C.

Clinton H. Whitehurst, Jr., is a professor of industrial management at Clemson University.

ISBN 0-8447-3221-4

Domestic Affairs Study 48, October 1976

Library of Congress Catalog Card No. 76-28670

Printed in the United States of America

CONTENTS

PREFACE

The Defense Transportation System is big business—affected by inflation, the energy shortage, and the changes taking place in the commercial transportation industry. It is imperative that we keep pace with these changes to ensure the Department of Defense will be able to respond to an emergency anywhere in the world.

Paul H. Riley, Deputy Assistant Secretary of Defense (Installations and Logistics), *Defense Transportation Journal,* December 1975.

This study examines the problem of how best to meet Department of Defense transportation requirements in an era of constricted defense budgets. The citation from Paul Riley's article, "DOD Transportation: Management Problems and the Search for Solutions," states an excellent justification for undertaking work in the area.

The recurring question addressed in this study is whether the Department of Defense can rely entirely upon the private sector for its peacetime and contingency transportation needs or whether it needs some capability of its own. (It is assumed that in a full mobilization all U.S. transportation assets would come under the direct operational control of one or more agencies of the federal government.) This issue has been raised indirectly by industry spokesmen, members of Congress, and officials within the executive branch of the federal government since the end of World War II. It is posed directly and explicitly in this study.

Components of the defense transportation system are examined in separate chapters. There are also discussions of the merchant marine as a naval auxiliary, of intermodal transportation, and of naval shipyards as a part of our peacetime mobilization base. Concluding chapters summarize these analyses and offer recommendations and suggestions. An examination of the historical background of the present defense transportation system is offered under the assumption that before a good decision can be made with respect to where we should go, it is important to understand where we have been.

Defense transportation is a complex subject, with policy determined as much by politics as by economics and strategic considerations. No single book could possibly consider every aspect of the topic. For this reason, the work is heavily, some might say excessively, documented. Such footnoting not only serves to authenticate data but, equally important, provides references for further research.

This study should not be considered one more attempt to cut the defense budget indiscriminately. The author's position for many years in favor of a second-to-none defense establishment is a matter of record. However, as Riley points out, defense transportation is big business. As such it should be thoroughly scrutinized to achieve efficiencies and savings wherever possible. To avoid such scrutiny would ill serve the national interest.

Many of the concepts in this study were developed from classroom discussions with graduate and undergraduate students about defense and transportation economics. A number of the arguments can be traced to the author's own background as a merchant marine and naval reserve officer. Ideas and suggestions have also been contributed by colleague members of the ad hoc Defense Studies Group at Clemson University and the two first readers of the paper, Hugh H. Macaulay and T. Bruce Yandle of Clemson's Department of Economics. Another source of invaluable advice and assistance was the Transportation Readiness Group of the U.S. General Accounting Office in Washington, D.C., a group in which the author had the privilege of serving in 1974–75. The assistance of Professor Frank Himsworth in the earlier stages of manuscript preparation and the most valuable contribution of the author's research assistant, Robert Fairey should also be acknowledged. Sincere appreciation is due to the secretarial staff of the Department of Industrial Management. Finally, errors of fact and logic should be attributed solely to the author.

1

INTRODUCTION

Unlike many world powers, the United States relies primarily upon privately owned commercial and industrial firms to provide military hardware, supplies, and services, both in peace and in war. Firms such as General Motors, Boeing, and the Newport News shipyard produce U.S. ships, planes, and tanks, and the privately owned merchant marine, railroads, and airlines move most equipment and men in a time of mobilization.

Procurement procedures are designed to meet military requirements at the lowest price possible. Congressional oversight in this respect is continuous. The investigative arm of Congress, the U.S. General Accounting Office, devotes considerable effort to auditing Department of Defense (DOD) programs, financial transactions, and overall management efficiency.

Although it cannot be proved in a strict accounting sense, United States reliance on its private sector for war materiel may be assumed to be as efficient economically as maintaining a state-owned armaments base. In fact, considerable evidence indicates the American system is superior, in spite of the well-documented cost overruns of many military purchases.[1]

The Department of Defense Budget

Although it is generally accepted that American reliance upon the private sector for its military needs is a reasonable option, there is no

---

[1] A case in point was the multibillion-dollar sale of General Dynamics' F-16, a general-purpose fighter plane, to Belgium, the Netherlands, Denmark, and Norway—the so-called arms deal of the century. The plane was in competition with entries from France and Sweden. Plane cost reportedly was a major determinant in the final selection.

1

Table 1

DEPARTMENT OF DEFENSE EXPENDITURES, SELECTED FISCAL YEARS, 1964–77

(in millions of dollars)

Fiscal Year	Amounts
1964	$ 50,665
1968	75,597
1974	84,992
1975	88,993
1976	98,261
1977	112,709

Source: U.S. Department of Defense, *Annual Defense Department Reports for FY 1976 and FY 1977.*

consensus with respect to the amount spent for defense purposes. In terms of 1976 dollars, the Department of Defense budget as measured in total obligational authority rose from $75.6 billion in fiscal year (FY) 1968—the high point of the Vietnam buildup—to a record proposed $112.7 billion for FY 1977. Table 1 indicates this increase and, for comparison, includes a pre-Vietnam year—FY 1964.

Mounting criticism of a seemingly ever-increasing DOD budget, particularly after American forces left Vietnam, prompted the Department of Defense in 1972 to publish an in-depth economic analysis of defense spending.[2] Its purpose was to point out that *in real terms* DOD budgets were becoming smaller, not larger. In turn, Senator William Proxmire (Democrat, Wisconsin), chairman of the Joint Economic Committee, requested a General Accounting Office (GAO) review of the methodology and conclusions of the DOD study. The GAO report found that FY 1973 defense expenditures were in real terms the smallest in nine years. It disagreed, however, with DOD's contention that the budget was the smallest in twenty-two years.[3]

Neither the DOD analysis nor the subsequent GAO review has stilled the debate. Those favoring reduced defense budgets remain convinced that significant cuts can be made without weakening

---

[2] U.S. Department of Defense, *The Economics of Defense Spending—A Look at the Realities* (Washington, D.C.: U.S. Government Printing Office, 1972).

[3] Comptroller General of the United States, *Comments on the Department of Defense Report "The Economics of Defense Spending—A Look at the Realities"* (Washington, D.C.: U.S. General Accounting Office, 1972).

military muscle.[4] On the other hand, many in and out of Congress accept DOD's view and see further cuts as endangering the national security. There is no disagreement, however, that the Department of Defense budget is indeed large and an attractive target when Congress considers overall federal spending.

The Logistics Share of the Budget

Logistics is a term that does not lend itself to precise definition.[5] In World War II, Admiral Ernest J. King reportedly said, "I don't know what the hell this logistics is that [General George C.] Marshall is always talking about but I want some of it."[6] One definition was provided by a 1970 blue ribbon panel set up to review the entire organization, structure, and operation of the Department of Defense. It defined logistics as "encompassing the management of all classes of U.S. military consumable supplies and secondary items world wide, depot maintenance, and overhaul of military equipment, plus transportation and traffic management."[7]

A good brief definition comes from the Logistics and Communications Division of the U.S. General Accounting Office, "logistics means providing all the material and services that a military force needs in peace or war" and adds that logistics "is the bridge between the combat troops and the industry and natural resources of our nation."[8]

The amount of the DOD budget devoted to logistics is not insignificant. Vice Admiral Thomas R. Weschler, director for logistics, Organization of the Joint Chiefs of Staff, estimates that 55 percent of

---

[4] This defense-economizing environment has been described as follows: "a fundamental change in national opinion has occurred in the United States in recent years, particularly toward the larger military issues. The change is rooted in a reorientation of national priorities from foreign matters to domestic needs [and] this new order may be with us for an extended period of time." See Murray L. Weidenbaum, *The Economics of Peacetime Defense* (New York: Praeger, 1972), p. 156.

[5] *Webster's Third New International Dictionary of the English Language Unabridged* (Springfield, Mass.: G. & C. Merriam Company, 1966) defines logistics as "military science in its planning and handling and implementation of personnel (as in classification, movement, evacuation) and material (as in production, distribution, maintenance) and facilities (as in construction, operations, distribution) and other related fields."

[6] Quoted in U.S. General Accounting Office, *Welcome to the Logistics & Communications Division* (1974), p. 2.

[7] Blue Ribbon Defense Panel, *Report to the President and the Secretary of Defense on the Department of Defense* (Washington, D.C.: U.S. Government Printing Office, July 1970), p. 97.

[8] General Accounting Office, *Welcome to Logistics*, pp. 2–3.

the DOD payroll, military and civilian, and 50 percent of the DOD budget are dedicated to logistics. He defines the mission of the military logistician as "trying to squeeze down the 50 percent of the defense budget dedicated to logistics so that we can either hold steady or build up the combat arm's share." He concludes that "only by cutting dollars in our support and logistics area will we have sufficient dollars to procure and support the B-1 or Trident or other such systems that are so very vital to keeping the peace."[9]

Obviously a large share of the DOD logistics budget is devoted to transportation. Paul Riley, deputy assistant secretary of defense, stated that approximately 40 million short tons of DOD cargo were moved in FY 1974 at an estimated cost of $3.5 billion.[10] This amount paid only for transportation services. Not included was DOD's very large capital investment in transportation hardware and facilities.

Defense Transportation Resources

DOD transportation requirements are provided by the Military Airlift Command (MAC), the Military Sealift Command (MSC), and the Military Traffic Management Command (MTMC), which has responsibility for procuring land transportation. These commands operate under the Departments of the Air Force, Navy, and Army, respectively. Each command acts as the single manager for the particular transportation provided and either purchases transportation service from commercial carriers or arranges shipment via DOD organic transportation systems.

Regarding transportation hardware and facilities procurement, the air force does not build its own planes, or the army its tanks, but the navy does operate naval shipyards under its Navy Materials Command.[11] The Military Traffic Management Command owns and operates several ocean terminals dedicated to handling defense cargoes.[12] The Military Airlift Command operates seventeen aerial ports—air force bases under MAC operational control that can handle the full range of DOD air freight and passenger movement require-

---

[9] Thomas R. Weschler, "Decade of Logistics," *Army Logistician*, vol. 7, no. 1 (January–February 1975), pp. 3, 5.

[10] Paul H. Riley, "DOD Transportation: Management Problems and the Search for Solutions," *Defense Management Journal*, vol. 11, no. 2 (April 1975), p. 2.

[11] The commander, Naval Ship Systems Command, acts as coordinator of all naval shipbuilding, conversion, and repair.

[12] The navy also operates two major port facilities for cargo ships and three ammunition ports in connection with Naval Ammunition Depots. These three are common-user ports.

ments. Six of these seventeen aerial ports are in the continental United States and one each in Hawaii and Guam.

Although MTMC, MAC, and the navy operate their own shipping terminals, aerial ports, and shipyards, the navy and MTMC in particular rely extensively on counterpart resources in the private sector. New navy construction is entirely in civilian-owned yards, and the bulk of MTMC-directed ocean cargo passes through civilian piers and container terminals.

In summary, the Department of Defense maintains a significant transport capability by operating its own air freight and passenger service (MAC), a shipping firm (MSC), and a fleet of railroad cars and a container service (MTMC). On the facilities side, the navy owns and operates shipyards, MTMC operates ocean terminals, and MAC operates a number of aerial ports. Thus some duplication between military and civilian transportation resources exists and has existed for a long time.

This duplication, however, has not been unnoticed and without critics. The size and scope of responsibility of DOD's merchant marine is monitored continuously by private industry and Congress. Few congressional hearings on merchant marine affairs omit a review of MSC policies and operations. Periodically, bills are introduced to shift more DOD cargo from MAC routes to civilian airlines. Over the years, the role of the naval shipyards, particularly insofar as they compete for business with their civilian counterparts, has often been the subject of heated debate.

Conclusion

Department of Defense spokesmen often and strenuously affirm the department's reliance on commercial transportation resources. Deputy Assistant Secretary of Defense Riley recently emphasized that "one of our major goals is to encourage the existence of a large, viable, U.S. commercial transportation system involving all modes of transport to meet the demands of DOD and the Nation in the event of a national emergency."[13] Acting Assistant Secretary of Defense John J. Bennett said:

> First, I cannot overemphasize that the Department of Defense (DOD) supports and needs a viable U.S. flag merchant marine in peace and war.

---

[13] Riley, "DOD Transportation," p. 2.

In a major war, Defense would be almost entirely reliant on civilian shipping assets. In peacetime, the need is no less great, where the vast preponderance of our Defense cargo moves in U.S. flag vessels, much of it in berth line service, side by side with the freight of U.S. commerce.[14]

And in a signed article, Major General Paul F. Patch, director of transportation, U.S. Air Force, asserted: "For the past two decades, the Air Force and the commercial air carrier industry have been joined in a partnership in which the commercial carriers augment the military capability not only in peacetime but also and more importantly during emergencies."[15]

Similar messages are repeated many times each year by DOD representatives in testimony before various congressional committees. Yet, as pointed out above, DOD *does* maintain an organic transportation capability, one that exists alongside similar privately owned resources. Some DOD transportation systems date from the eighteenth and nineteenth centuries.

The Department of Defense offers a detailed and complex rationale for owning and operating its own transportation system, which will be treated in the relevant chapters of this study. With logistics accounting for half the DOD budget, however, and with transportation accounting for much of the logistics expenditures, it is fair to question whether DOD could not rely on the commercial sector for its transportation needs either completely or to a greater extent than it does. The main purpose of this study is to examine the components of the defense transportation system, to question their reasons for being, and to assess the capabilities of the private sector to assume a greater share, if not all, of this role. In addition, several transportation-related areas in which possible savings may be realized will also be reviewed.

While an assumption of this study will be that privately owned transportation enterprises are more cost-effective than a DOD in-house capability, it is also recognized that strategic mobility is a cornerstone of present defense planning. It follows, therefore, that nothing must impair the ability of our transportation system to respond quickly and effectively to any threat to American interests anywhere in the world. That, too, is an accepted assumption of the paper.

---

[14] Testimony of John J. Bennett before the Merchant Marine Subcommittee of the House Committee on Merchant Marine and Fisheries, June 5, 1975.

[15] Paul F. Patch, "Airlift Enhancement," *Translog: The Journal of Military Transportation Management*, vol. 5 (June 1974), p. 3.

2

THE DEFENSE TRANSPORTATION SYSTEM SINCE 1776

The word *logistics* enjoys a vogue in American colleges of business and management. New textbooks on the subject are being written, and new courses are being offered. Moreover, texts and courses in transportation rarely fail to devote considerable attention to the logistics problems of corporate America.

Though business schools and the private sector itself may only recently have discovered logistics to be worthy of their attention, the military planners and tacticians have long been aware of the subject. The well-planned and constructed roads of ancient Rome may well have served commerce, but their chief purpose was to provide an unmatched mobility for Roman legions and their logistical support. Roman military commanders seem to have understood well that logistics is the bridge between a nation's combat troops and its industry and natural resources. If anything, logistics is more important today than in time past.

This chapter looks at the historic development of a key element in logistics planning—transportation. Present-day military transportation commands—the Military Sealift Command, the Military Airlift Command, and the Military Traffic Management Command—are briefly outlined. The role of the merchant marine as a naval auxiliary and the development of naval shipyards are also traced.

The Revolution and the Nineteenth Century

The American Revolution. With the advent of war, the American colonies faced logistical problems of staggering proportions. They lacked a transportation system that would allow distant colonies to support one another as the military situation required. Often, one area enjoyed relative abundance while another suffered shortages of crisis proportions. Since the earliest settlements, the colonists had a most efficient ocean transportation system, but, with the outbreak of hostilities, this system was denied to them by blockading British warships. The ocean system had worked so well it discouraged investment in more costly roads. The price exacted from the colonies for this unbalanced system was high. Professor James A. Huston, in his authoritative work on the history of army logistics, states the fundamental nature of the problem.

> Undoubtedly the greatest advantage the British enjoyed in the Revolutionary War was control of the sea, not only because it enabled them to keep open their own communications with the homeland, but because of its special significance in a war against a country whose poorly developed internal transportation forced it to rely heavily on coasting vessels for transportation from one region to another. With the use of coastwise sea lanes denied the Americans much of the time, while open to the British, Northern and Southern states found mutual support generally impracticable.[1]

During the revolution, logistical support for military operations was, as often as not, in civilian hands. The navy had difficulty enough keeping its few warships at sea without developing its own merchant marine.[2] Most naval officers and crews came from the civilian merchant marine in the early years of the war. The army also relied heavily on civilian transportation. When possible, civilian drivers were hired for transportation service including drivers for artillery horses. Typically, civilian labor was engaged for a specified term or for a particular job.[3]

Military transportation in the revolution suffered from two handicaps. The lack of a land transportation system probably was the most important cause of the well-documented hardships and lost opportunities experienced by American forces. The second handicap was the Americans' extremely austere financial condition. With little money and credit, the War Department simply did not have the funds to develop a military transportation system. Army engineers built and

---

[1] James A. Huston, *The Sinews of War: Army Logistics 1775–1953*, Army Historical Series, vol. 2 (Washington, D.C.: U.S. Government Printing Office, 1966), p. 34.

[2] Merchant ships fitted out as privateers provided a needed morale boost in the opening years of the war. In 1776, 229 ships were captured, and in 1777 the number was 331. See E. B. Potter, *The Naval Academy Illustrated History of the U.S. Navy* (New York: Crowell Press, 1971), p. 9.

[3] Huston, *The Sinews of War*, p. 35.

maintained a few roads, and the military made use of whatever was available, most of which was supplied (or requisitioned) from the private sector of the economy.

After the war, by an act of Congress on April 30, 1798, the Navy Department was created. During the Naval War with France (1798–99) Secretary of the Navy Benjamin Stoddert urged the building of naval yards at a number of strategic locations. In February 1799 he was directed to have constructed two "docks" for the repair and outfitting of naval vessels, with an appropriation of $50,000. The Portsmouth, N.H., yard was established in 1800 and the Philadelphia yard in 1801. By 1806 four additional yards had been built at Charleston (Boston), Mass.; Brooklyn, N.Y.; Norfolk, Va., and Washington, D.C.

President Jefferson did not believe an active navy was necessary in peacetime and proposed that, as an economy measure, a huge drydock be constructed, capable of handling the twelve frigates that then composed the fleet. With the ships drydocked, the crews could be discharged.[4] This earlier-day "mothball fleet" idea, however, did not carry in Congress.

The War of 1812. Many of the logistical problems that beset the Americans during the Revolution reappeared during the War of 1812. Once again a British navy was able to disrupt, almost at will, ocean transportation along the East Coast and Gulf Coast. Interior transportation, though much improved by road construction during the so-called Turnpike Era, was still unsatisfactory in much of the old Northwest.[5] In many places, supplies could move only along inland rivers.

Though British warships prevailed in a strategic sense along the American coast, armed American merchant ships prevailed in an economic sense elsewhere. These "privateers"—civilian-owned and manned—wreaked havoc on English commerce. They operated under a "letter of marque," a license issued by the government of the flag they flew. Amounts realized by captures of enemy shipping were divided between the vessel and the government, but the vessel's owner bore the entire cost of arming, fitting out, and manning the privateer.

Privateers were a major cause of English willingness to negotiate

---

[4] Eugene J. Peltier, *The Bureau of Yards and Docks of the Navy and the Civil Engineer Corps* (New York: The Newcomen Society in North America, 1961), p. 8.

[5] For a discussion of road construction in the period, see D. Philip Locklin, *Economics of Transportation* (Homewood, Ill.: Richard D. Irwin, Inc., 1972), pp. 102–105. Note that the Cumberland Road did not extend into the old Northwest until after 1820.

an end to the war. Edgar Stanton Maclay, in his extensive work on American privateers, notes that the 515 privateers commissioned by the United States during the conflict were credited with 1,345 known captures.[6] The effect of their operations can be judged by examining increases in prices in Great Britain. In June 1813 the price of flour had risen threefold to $58 a barrel, beef to $38, and pork to $36. Lumber was selling at $72 per 1,000 feet. Maclay quotes a resolution adopted in September 1814 at a public meeting in Glasgow:

> The number of privateers with which our channels have been infested, the audacity with which they have approached our coasts, and the success with which their enterprise has been attended, have proved injurious to our commerce, humbling to our pride and discreditable to the directors of the naval power of the British nation . . . that there is reason to believe that in the short space of less than 24 months above eight hundred vessels have been captured by that power whose maritime strength we have hitherto, impolitically held in contempt.[7]

The War of 1812 illustrated what could be accomplished by a merchant marine acting as a naval auxiliary in support of the national interest. Seventy-five years later, Alfred Thayer Mahan in his classic *The Influence of Seapower Upon History* (1890) pointed out the vital relationship between the navy and merchant marine. In commenting upon the French navy under Louis XIV, he questioned whether a navy can exist without merchant shipping.

> Can this navy be had without restoring the merchant shipping? It is doubtful. History has proved that such a purely military seapower can be built up by a despot, as was done by Louis XIV; but though so fair seeming, experience showed that his navy was like a growth which having no root soon withers away.[8]

For centuries the British have understood that a continuing commercial maritime environment—including not only shipping but also shipyards, fisheries, supporting industries, and educational institutions—is essential in developing seapower to its fullest. The Soviet Union is learning that lesson rapidly.

---

[6] Edgar S. Maclay, *A History of American Privateers* (Freeport, N.Y.: Books for Libraries Press, 1899), p. 506. For a less charitable view of privateering, see "The Birth of a Navy," *U.S. Naval Institute Proceedings*, vol. 101 (October 1975), p. 21.

[7] Ibid., pp. xv–xvi.

[8] Alfred Thayer Mahan, *The Influence of Sea Power Upon History; 1660–1783*, Louis M. Thacker, American Century Series (New York: Sagamore Press, 1957), p. 75.

The War with Mexico. In the 1840s, a conflict with Mexico loomed, and the War Department began mobilization preparations. The Second Seminole War had only recently been brought to a conclusion in 1842. In that war, as in the war with Mexico, initial army transportation requirements were met by the private sector. Chartered sailing ships, steamers, and riverboats transported the armies to their staging areas in Florida, Texas, and Mexico, and supported the military effort by transporting materiel and supplies. In these conflicts, unlike the earlier wars with England, the United States was able to utilize an ocean transportation system effectively.

In the Mexican War, the army acquired a sizable sea transportation service and expanded its inland transportation capability, that is, its wagon inventory. At the conclusion of hostilities, however, Quartermaster General Thomas S. Jesup decided against having the army maintain its large transportation capability. He quickly disposed of most of his vessels and proposed that the navy accept responsibility for all ocean transportation—for the army as well as the navy. In effect, he anticipated an action that would take place a century later. He judged it more economical to hire private transportation for land movement than to maintain government equipment. By 1849, contract freighting had been introduced in the West, and the army's merchant marine was down to fifteen vessels.[9]

The Civil War. The Civil War was the most bitterly contested and bloody conflict in the nation's history and its first experience with total war. Being a total war, it became an organized war.[10] It spurred the development by the War and Navy Departments of a large commercial-like transportation capability. It was also the first war in which railroads played a major role.

As in the past, transportation responsibilities in both North and South fell upon the private sector at the beginning of hostilities. On both sides, private enterprise responded well. The development of the Union military transport system, however, is of chief interest here because precedents were set which extend to World War II and beyond. And, although private transportation responded fully to the demands made upon it, the North needed more of everything than the system could provide, particularly when the Union armies advanced into the Confederacy and had to construct military railroads.[11] Civil War

---

[9] Huston, *The Sinews of War*, p. 155.

[10] In considering the Civil War as an organized war, see Allan Nevins, *The War for the Union*, vol. 3, *The Organized War 1863–64* (New York: Charles Scribner's Sons, 1971).

[11] Ibid., p. 300.

historian Allan Nevins has high praise for the part the privately owned railroads played in the conflict, pointing out that although the U.S. superintendent of railroads had the authority to operate all systems, this power of seizure was used in only a few emergencies.[12] Also of major logistical importance to the Union were the inland waterway and ocean transportation systems. As with railroads, the private sector was responsive but lacked overall capacity and could not meet special requirements.

The North's merchant marine primarily carried on the nation's commerce and secondarily provided men and ships to support the armies in the field and the blockade of the South. In the South, insofar as a merchant marine existed, its role was blockade running.

As in the Mexican conflict, the War and Navy Departments provided for their water transport separately. The navy built and operated a fleet of supply ships to support its blockading squadrons. Nevins describes these supply steamers as "roomy, fast vessels with capacious ice houses which could hold 35,000 pounds of fresh beef." In addition they transported vegetables, stores, mail, and passengers between East Coast ports and the blockading squadrons.[13] On the army side, by November 1864, the Quartermaster Department was operating "a huge fleet of transports, including 39 ocean steamers, and many scores of river and bay steamers, steam tug-boats, barks, brigs, and other vessels and chartering as well 74 additional ocean steamers, 164 river and bay steamers, and several hundred other ships."[14]

There was also a rapid buildup of naval shipyard capacity for new construction, repair, and overhaul during the Civil War. As in the case of the railroads and inland waterways, the private sector responded willingly but could not meet the need to quadruple its shipbuilding and ship repair capacity almost overnight. Expansion of existing naval yards was held to be the best way to go.

The Spanish-American War. At the beginning of the Spanish-American War in 1898 the "Army had neither an ocean-going vessel nor experience in operating transports."[15] Such a deficiency was

---

[12] Ibid., p. 302. Actually, the authority for the President to seize the railroads was granted by Congress in January 1862, and in May of that year President Lincoln formally took possession of them, though operation by and large remained with the individual firms.

[13] Ibid., p. 286.

[14] Ibid., p. 294. For a good description of the role of river transportation in the Civil War, see also Huston, *The Sinews of War*, pp. 211–214.

[15] Huston, *The Sinews of War*, p. 282.

critical since the conflict was entirely an overseas war, with the main theaters in Cuba, Puerto Rico, and the Philippines. Again civilian ships were pressed into service. Cargo vessels were chartered and converted to troop ships.

Railroads again bore the main burden of inland movement of men and supplies. Initially the task was to move men and materiel to Tampa, Florida, for embarkation to Cuba. Unfortunately, this port city on Florida's west coast lacked facilities to handle the large numbers of troops and mountains of supplies that poured in. As Professor Huston notes:

> The two railroads serving the Tampa area were soon clogged with freight cars. Facilities and wagons were lacking for rapid unloading, and many cars arrived without invoices or bills of lading, so that their contents could be determined only by personal inspection. Within a few weeks a thousand cars were backed up on sidings as far away as Columbia, South Carolina . . .[16]

The problem of obtaining necessary shipping was magnified tenfold in the Pacific. Sufficient shipping was simply not available. In due course, however, a fleet of transports and supply ships was chartered and purchased, and sailed to Manila. One hundred ten days after hostilities began, the war ended.

World War I and the Interwar Period

Two transportation events of note occurred after the war with Spain and before U.S. entry into World War I. One was the formation of the Army Transport Service (ATS) in 1898, with an initial purchase of six British ships.[17] The first mission of ATS was to move and support American forces during the Philippine Insurrection. Eventually the ATS fleet numbered 125 chartered or owned vessels. The second event of note was the introduction of motor vehicles—primarily trucks—into the army's logistical support inventory. They were of commercial design and widely used in General Pershing's expedition into Mexico in 1916.

World War I. Between 1820 and 1860, 77 percent of American cargoes had been carried in American vessels. By 1910 the figure had declined to 9 percent. The United States had become almost com-

---

[16] Ibid., pp. 280–281.

[17] Carl E. McDowell and Helen M. Gibbs, *Ocean Transportation* (New York: McGraw-Hill Book Company, Inc., 1954), p. 458.

pletely dependent on foreign shipping. At the beginning of World War I, however, foreign shipping returned home and there was no American tonnage to take its place. Freight rates on cotton from a southern U.S. port to the United Kingdom rose from $2.50 to $60 a bale and wheat from 5 cents to 60 cents a bushel.[18]

Meeting wartime shipping needs. At the urging of President Wilson, Congress passed the Shipping Act of 1916. It established a U.S. Shipping Board "for the purpose of encouraging, developing and creating a naval auxiliary and naval reserve and a merchant marine" to meet the commercial requirements of the United States.[19] Upon American entry into World War I, the Shipping Board set up a government-owned corporation—the Emergency Fleet Corporation—to build and operate merchant ships.

At the commencement of hostilities, the army was operating its own troop and cargo ships. These vessels carried civilian crews, but crew shortages and lack of discipline plagued the operation almost from the outset. The army finally turned over the operation of most of its shipping to the navy, first the transports and then the cargo vessels.[20] Two years earlier the quartermaster general had attempted to "militarize" the Army Transport Service by operating the vessels with regular army personnel, but his proposal was not implemented. In any event, the navy now assumed responsibility not only for its own logistical support but for much of the army's requirements as well. To handle this task, the Naval Overseas Transport Service was established. In November 1918, it was operating 321 ships, including 94 supplied by the Emergency Fleet Corporation.[21]

Throughout the war, merchant shipping was in short supply, particularly by mid-1917, as submarine losses mounted and the American deployment to Europe increased. To avoid conflict among the War and Navy Departments, the War Industries Board, and other government agencies, control of all American-flag shipping was passed to the Shipping Board in August 1917. The problem was where to obtain more ships. An obvious possibility was to build them, and a gigantic shipbuilding program was launched. Another source was the

[18] Edmund A. Walsh, *Ships and National Safety: The Role of the Merchant Marine in a Balanced Economy* (Washington, D.C.: Georgetown University Press, 1934), p. 8.

[19] U.S. Congress, *Shipping Act of 1916*, Public Law No. 260, 64th Cong., 1st sess., 1917, p. 1.

[20] The army did not consider this transfer of responsibility permanent but only a wartime expedient. See Huston, *The Sinews of War*, p. 353.

[21] Donald W. Mitchell, *History of the Modern American Navy* (New York: Alfred A. Knopf, 1946), p. 237.

enemy shipping seized in American ports, which also added valuable tonnage. Still more could be obtained by confiscating neutral shipping. This policy was implemented reluctantly in 1918 and yielded approximately 1 million gross tons.

The American merchant marine was even less prepared for World War I than were the armed services.[22] As noted earlier, only 9 percent of American trade was being carried by U.S.-flag vessels in 1910. After 1914, however, and prior to American entry into the conflict, the U.S. merchant fleet was expanded significantly by the transfer of foreign flag shipping to American registry. Yet, a wartime American merchant marine on the scale visualized by Shipping Board planners never materialized. In fact, only a sixth of the 3,000 ships authorized by the board for construction were completed before the armistice. In May 1922, the program ended, after having spent $3.3 billion. The United States now had a huge merchant marine, some 13.5 million tons, half of it government-owned.[23] Privately owned American shipping also made a substantial contribution, but the war ended before its resources could be totally mobilized. The British merchant service, then the world's largest, played the dominant shipping role in the war.

Land transportation. In the continental United States, railroads met the great bulk of inland transportation requirements. Rail coordination was directed from Washington, D.C., by the American Railway Association, which served as a de facto coordinating committee. As mobilization demands increased, railroads were constantly barraged by claims for transportation priorities, not only from the army and navy, but also from the many government boards, such as the Munitions Board, set up to marshal the nation's resources. Delays and congestion increased, and in December 1917—eight months after the U.S. declaration of war—the railroads were taken over by presidential proclamation. The secretary of the Treasury was designated director of railroads, and the U.S. Railroad Administration was created to run the nationwide system. Unlike the experience of the Civil War, when railroad administration was left in the hands of the companies, the 1917 takeover was complete. The day-to-day task of operating the system fell to the army.

---

[22] Caution should be used, however, in defining "preparedness." Military materiel in 1917 was not as specialized as in the 1970s. Murray L. Weidenbaum notes that "At the outbreak of World War I, four fifths or more of the equipment of the armies that took the field consisted of standard peacetime goods produced in ordinary civilian facilities." See Murray L. Weidenbaum, *The Economics of Peacetime Defense* (New York: Praeger, 1972), p. 134.

[23] Samuel A. Lawrence, *U.S. Merchant Shipping Policies and Politics* (Washington, D.C.: Brookings Institution, 1966), p. 40.

Whether the 1917 government seizure was precipitate has been a matter of continuing debate. The experience of World War II suggests that the action was hasty and that the major problems could have been resolved without it. Delays and congestion did occur on a large scale, however, and the situation was certainly critical. Judgment at the time favored strong, centralized railroad administration, and government control seemed the best means of achieving that goal.

As in previous wars, the service most involved with railroads in World War I was the army. The movement by rail of vast quantities of supplies and thousands of troops to eastern embarkation ports was a logistics task of monumental proportions. Moreover, lack of coordination contributed to delays and congestion. Early in 1918, the army organized an Inland Traffic Service to coordinate all military shipments. The army also established the Embarkation Service to direct the movement overseas of troops, equipment, and supplies from East Coast ports. The service assumed control of these ports, with authority over piers and warehouses as well as troop-support facilities in the embarkation area. After the war, in 1919, the two services were consolidated into the Transportation Service. The present Military Traffic Management Command is the lineal descendant of that organization.

After the War. The end of World War I found the government in control of U.S. railroads and the owner of one of the largest merchant fleets in the world. What to do with this massive transportation inventory, particularly the merchant marine, became the subject of lengthy congressional debate.

A decision on railroads was reached with passage of the Transportation Act of 1920. Although nationalization was rejected, the act effectively established the principle of strict government control over railroad operations. It was control with a vengeance. Restrictive provisions of the legislation left the railroads privately owned in name only. *Direct* government operation of the railroads, however, was terminated on March 1, 1920.

The merchant marine posed a more complex problem because the federal government had become deeply involved in the shipping business. Many members of the Congress wanted this huge fleet, built with the taxpayers' money, to be operated by the government for profit, but others strongly opposed a government-controlled shipping operation. The Merchant Marine Act of 1920 favored private ownership, though not decisively. The preamble to the act states:

16

It is necessary for the national defense and for the proper growth of its foreign and domestic commerce that the United States shall have a merchant marine of the best equipped and most suitable types of vessels sufficient to carry the greater part of its commerce and serve as a naval or military auxiliary in time of war or national emergency.[24]

It is noteworthy that the reference was not to a "privately owned merchant marine," but merely to a "merchant marine." The legislation provided for the sale of government-owned ships. It allowed the government to establish service on routes it deemed desirable with government-owned ships and to offer these ships and routes for sale. The legislation also provided a modest construction loan fund and maintained subsidization of ocean shipping under the Ocean Mail Act of 1891.

The Merchant Marine Act of 1928 replaced the limited mail subsidies established in 1891 with a broad system of mail contract awards. The law also increased federal funding for new ship construction and reconditioning.

The most comprehensive piece of maritime legislation in American history was the Merchant Marine Act of 1936. Its provisions and philosophy remain the basic maritime policy today. Of particular interest is the part of Title I that states, "the United States shall have a merchant marine owned and operated . . . by *citizens of the United States* [italics added] insofar as may be practicable."[25] The concept of a privately owned merchant marine was now firmly established.

Changing economic conditions in land transportation—resulting particularly from the rise of motor transport—and the advent of the depression in the 1930s disclosed a number of weaknesses in the Transportation Act of 1920. Several provisions restricting railroad operations were repealed in 1933. The Transportation Act of 1940 further increased the freedom of railroad management and brought government policy toward railroads more in line with that toward other carriers. Once more, the railroad industry could be considered privately owned and operated.

From World War II to the Present

World War II. A major problem in this war, as in World War I, was how to move sufficient tonnage by sea, land, and air.

---

24 U.S. Congress, *Merchant Marine Act of 1920*, Public Law No. 261, 66th Cong., 1st sess., 1920, p. 1.

25 U.S. Congress, *Merchant Marine Act of 1936*, Public Law No. 835, 74th Cong., 1st sess., 1936, p. 1.

Maritime transportation. Although the navy took over responsibility for crews on army merchant-type ships during World War I, it was understood—by the army at least—that the arrangement was not permanent. The Army Transport Service continued to exist. In 1920 the Naval Overseas Transport Service became the Naval Transportation Service and was made permanent, though it was generally inactive until the outbreak of war in 1939. An effort was made in 1941 to have the navy man and operate ships of the Army Transport Service but the plan was not authorized.[26]

Coordination of merchant shipping came quickly following United States entry into World War II. In 1942, two months after Pearl Harbor, overall responsibility for allocating American tonnage was assigned to the War Shipping Administration. Though required to coordinate with this administration, the army kept control of its own vessels. This army fleet never exceeded 200 ships.

The most obvious solution to Allied supply problems was to build more ships. The Maritime Commission, an independent agency created by the Merchant Marine Act of 1936, was given the task. Between 1941 and 1945, more than 5,500 vessels of many designs were built, the most numerous being the well-known Liberty Ship. With the end of hostilities, the War Shipping Administration passed into history. In 1946 its responsibilities were either terminated or taken over by the Maritime Commission.

The Merchant Ship Sales Act of 1946 provided for the disposal of the war-accumulated inventory of government-owned ships, some 5,000 in all. By 1951, when the authority to sell these vessels ended, government holdings were down to approximately 1,800 ships, laid up at a number of sites on the East, Gulf, and Pacific coasts. By terms of the 1946 legislation, this tonnage became part of the National Defense Reserve Fleet. Responsibility for its maintenance was assigned to the Maritime Commission.

Land and air transportation. While the army continued to operate a number of ships, even though the great bulk of its ocean transportation needs was met by the merchant marine, its major World War II logistics role was in other areas. As in World War I, it had responsibility for managing ports of embarkation. The task was specifically assigned to the war-created Transportation Corps, whose mission in this respect was essentially that of the earlier Embarkation Service.

Whether the government should again take over operation of the railroads was considered briefly. The answer was never seriously in doubt, largely because from the outset the railroads, under private

---

[26] McDowell and Gibbs, *Ocean Transportation*, p. 459.

management, did all that was required and more. Equally important was the realization that government operation of the railroads in World War I left much to be desired. Military input to railroad operations was channeled through the army's Transportation Corps. Other agencies, including the Association of American Railroads, the Office of Defense Transportation, and the Interstate Commerce Commission cooperated to insure an efficient rail transportation system. Assisting in the inland movement of material and supplies were motor freight carriers, pipelines, and barge shipping, the latter contributing significantly in freight movement along the intercoastal waterway as well as on the older, established river systems. Coordinating these systems with military requirements was also a Transportation Corps responsibility. In addition to directing military traffic in the continental United States, the corps was given the task of building and maintaining military railroads overseas.

The first significant use of airplanes in the movement of men and materiel occurred in World War II. The most widely known military air service was the army air force's Air Transport Command. The number of tons moved by air was quite small compared with the total moved during the war, but, as a demonstration of what could be accomplished by this mode when other means were lacking, the results were impressive. In July 1945, the Air Transport Command was operating 3,700 planes worldwide. The lessons learned would prove invaluable during the Berlin airlift a few years later.

The navy also established an air arm for logistic support. Although not as large as the Air Transport Command or as well known, this service, the Naval Air Transport Service, performed essentially the same functions in moving men and materiel to destinations throughout the world. It operated 429 transport aircraft over a system of 63,000 route miles. The planes relied upon by both services were C-47s and C-54s (DC-3s and DC-4s). The navy also employed a number of stripped-down bomber and patrol planes, including Mariners and Liberators.

Throughout the war, both transport services depended heavily on commercial air carriers, generally through contracted services. Both commands were started with commercial planes and crews.

The Post-World War II World. The National Security Act of 1947 and amendments in 1949, which established the air force as a separate service and created the Department of Defense, paved the way for consolidation of military transportation responsibilities. In June 1948 the navy's Naval Air Transport Service and the air force's Air Transport Command, successor to the earlier Army Air Corps Command, combined to form the Military Air Transport Service (MATS). On October 1, 1949, the Military Sea Transport Service (MSTS) was created from the Naval Transport Service and the Army Transport Service. Transfer of army ships began in March 1950 and was completed within six months.

In 1948, when the Soviet Union imposed a land blockade on Berlin, the Allies considered sending armed military convoys by train and truck through East German check points but decided instead to airlift supplies to the beleaguered city. Thousands of flights were flown along air corridors between West Germany and Berlin by both military and civilian aircraft. U.S. civilian air carriers flew over 600 transatlantic flights and more than 2,500 flights through the German air corridors in support of the airlift program.

The Korean War. In June 1950—a little more than a year after the Berlin blockade was lifted—the United States intervened, with United Nations backing, in support of South Korea after it was attacked from the north. The newly created MSTS started with a fleet of 174 ships, including 50 transports, 48 tankers, and 25 cargo ships, and rapidly expanded its sealift capability with an additional 400 ships from the privately owned merchant marine and the National Defense Reserve Fleet.

The MATS effort was again supplemented by the civilian air carriers, which provided the greater portion of the Korean airlift. U.S.-flag carriers lifted 67 percent of the passengers, 56 percent of the freight, and 70 percent of the mail. They carried more than one-and-one-half times the combined total traffic moved by MATS, the Royal Canadian Air Force, the UN airlift, and foreign flag airlines.[27]

In 1951, the Civil Reserve Air Fleet (CRAF) was established by joint agreement of the secretaries of defense and commerce. This agreement provided a means for U.S. registered civilian aircraft to supplement MATS in an emergency.

Coordinating Land Transportation. Progressing at a slower pace, the army in 1951—three years after the creation of MATS and two years after MSTS came into existence—was given responsibility for military land transportation overseas. In 1956—when the secretary of the navy became the single manager of sealift, and the secretary of the air force of airlift—the secretary of the army was designated the single manager for traffic management in the United States. He was

---

[27] Paul R. Ignatius, "Let the Airlines Play an Optimum Role in Supporting National Defense," *Defense Management Journal*, vol. 11 (April 1975), p. 12.

to consolidate all land military traffic activities. Internally, responsibility fell to the newly created Military Traffic Management Agency. In a 1962 Department of Defense reorganization, this agency became the Defense Traffic Management Service. Two years later, it was succeeded by the Military Traffic Management and Terminal Service, when the army's authority was broadened to include military traffic, land transportation, and common user terminals.

The Vietnam War. American involvement in the Vietnam War again led to an increase in the size of the MSTS fleet. At the height of the conflict, it numbered 436 ships, including both government-owned and commercially chartered vessels and 176 vessels from the National Defense Reserve Fleet. During American military operations in Southeast Asia, more than 95 percent of the military cargo delivered there moved by sea.

The Military Air Transport Service also expanded its airlift capability during the Vietnam War, not only with its own increased capacity but also with the extensive use of commercial aircraft. During 1966, for example, U.S. airlines carried 90 percent of MATS passengers and 30 percent of MATS air cargo.

The 1973 Middle East War. On October 6, 1973, six days after Egypt launched an attack on Israel across the Suez Canal and Syria attacked on the Golan Heights, President Nixon ordered the resupply of Israeli forces. Between October 13 and November 14, 1973, the Military Airlift Command, the successor to the Military Air Transport Service, delivered 22,479 short tons of supplies to Israel. The C-5s demonstrated their ability to deliver outsize cargo, such as self-propelled guns and tanks, to a battle front thousands of miles away.[28] In this operation, unlike those in Berlin, Korea, and Vietnam, privately owned U.S. transport—air and sea—did not contribute to the American logistics effort. The airlift was flown by MAC planes supplemented by Israeli commercial aircraft. The sealift was accomplished primarily by nine Israeli-flag ships. U.S. commercial air carriers were opposed to committing their planes voluntarily to the resupply effort unless the Civil Reserve Air Fleet provisions were

---

[28] As impressive as the airlift was, in its review of the operation, the U.S. General Accounting Office pointed out that only 39 percent of the airlifted cargo was delivered before the cease-fire on October 24. The first ship arrived in Israel on November 2 with 3,321 short tons of outsize cargo. See Comptroller General of the United States, *Airlift Operations of the Military Airlift Command During the 1973 Middle East War* (Washington, D.C.: U.S. General Accounting Office, 1975), p. 8. When the general resupply of Israeli forces was completed in 1974, sealift accounted for 75 percent of the cargo moved.

invoked. These carriers were cautious because U.S. military aircraft were not operating in the war zone and also because they feared Arab economic retaliation.[29] The sealift resupply effort fell to Israeli-flag ships mainly because they were quickly made available. At the outbreak of hostilities, the MSC-controlled fleet was dispersed worldwide. In this respect, Lieutenant General Fred Kornet, Jr., the army's deputy chief of staff for logistics remarked: "Fortunately, in the October War, Israel provided the ships for the movement of sealifted cargo. If we had relied on the Military Sealift Command (MSC) controlled fleet to move that cargo, great difficulty would have been encountered and the overall success of the operation would have been significantly reduced."[30]

Present DOD transportation agencies. On June 30, 1974, the Military Sealift Command was operating ninety-six government-owned vessels and had an additional sixty-nine privately owned vessels on charter. On the air side, the Military Airlift Command had 535 aircraft in operation, 70 of which were C-5s and 234 C-141s. The Civil Reserve Air Fleet comprised 330 contractually committed commercial aircraft. Since the American disengagement from Vietnam, however, both the MSC-controlled fleet and the number of military planes assigned to MAC have decreased.

The Military Traffic Management Command, successor to the former Military Traffic Management and Terminal Service, does not control a complete transportation system, as do MSC and MAC.[31] It does control and direct a sizable amount of railroad rolling stock through its Defense Railway Interchange Fleet. In 1972, this fleet consisted of 4,921 cars—134 passenger cars, 950 box cars, 937 flat cars, and 2,900 tank cars. By early 1975, this total had dropped to 4,149 cars, of which 2,287 were tankers.[32] MTMC also has the responsibility for coordinating recommendations of the services on needs of the defense highway system. This command determines which needs are eligible for consideration under the Highways for National Defense Program. The Bureau of Public Roads and the

[29] Comptroller General, *Airlift Operations of the Military Airlift Command*, p. 7.

[30] Fred Kornet, Jr. "Strategic Mobility: The Army Perspective," *Defense Management Journal*, vol. 2 (April 1975), p. 17.

[31] The Military Air Transport Service (MATS) became the Military Airlift Command (MAC) on January 1, 1966. The Military Sea Transportation Service (MSTS) became the Military Sealift Command (MSC) on August 1, 1970. The Military Traffic Management and Terminal Service became the Military Traffic Management Command on July 31, 1974.

[32] *The Official Railway Equipment Register*, vol. 90 (New York: National Railway Publication Co., April 1975), p. 769.

military have cooperated on these needs since the early 1920s, when the bureau requested the War Department to designate highways of strategic importance in mobilization. Since highway administration is a shared function in the United States, MTMC must coordinate the movement of military traffic with state, county, and local jurisdictions as well as with the Bureau of Public Roads. Out of a total road mileage in the United States in 1969 of 3,161,726 miles, only 182,676 miles, or about 6 percent, were under federal control. These roads are located primarily in federal parks, forests, and reservations.[33]

Naval Shipyards. Operations at naval shipyards have varied through the years with mobilization requirements. By 1835, two conventional drydocks had been built at the Boston and Norfolk yards, and additional naval shipyards were constructed at Mare Island, Calif., in 1852 and at Puget Sound, Wash., in 1896. In the twentieth century, yards were established at Charleston, S.C.; Pearl Harbor, Hawaii; Long Beach, Calif.; and Hunters Point, Calif., in that order. Peak employment in all yards occurred during World War II, rising to 353,000 in July 1943. Then, employment dropped to 68,000 in May 1950, and increased to 98,000 during the Vietnam conflict. Employment was about 60,000 in March 1974.[34] Since the end of World War II, the Boston, Brooklyn, and Hunters Point yards have closed. The Washington, D.C., yard has not been used as a yard since World War I. Ship repair facilities at San Diego were closed in 1965.

As the number of naval ships decreased to the lowest point since before Pearl Harbor, competition for naval ship repair and overhaul contracts has increased significantly. There were 57 major private shipyards at the close of World War II, but by 1975 only 17 had survived. Six of these handle all new navy construction. The remaining major private yards, the naval shipyards, and some 175 smaller private yards divide approximately $1.2 billion annually in navy repair, alteration, and conversion work. Testimony before Congress on apportioning this expenditure has been bitter and acrimonious through the years. Representatives of private yards argue that they are more cost-efficient but will be forced to shut down without additional navy work, thereby decreasing the shipyard mobilization base. Spokesmen for the naval yards, on the other hand, offer a variety of reasons for keeping the larger share of the repair and overhaul budget. Extensive hearings on the status of U.S. shipyards—naval and private—were held before the Seapower

---

[33] Locklin, *Economics of Transportation*, p. 32.

[34] U.S. Congress, House, Seapower Subcommittee of the Committee on Armed Services, *Hearings on Current Status of Shipyards 1974, Part 1*, 93d Cong., 2d sess., July 1974, p. 108.

Subcommittee of the House Committee on the Armed Services in the summer and fall of 1974.

Conclusion

In times of mobilization, the United States has relied upon its civilian transportation industries as the base upon which military transportation systems have been built. In some periods the civilian system was taken over totally, as the railroads were in World War I. In other periods, military systems were manned by civilians, as army transports were in the nineteenth century. Typically, military transportation systems have been cut back following a war. Sometimes the organizational unit is abolished entirely or becomes inactive. This was generally the case after World War I. After World War II, however, large military transportation commands remained intact.

Admiral William Callaghan, first commander of the Military Sea Transportation Service and an advocate of a parallel military transport system, was asked in a congressional hearing in 1950 whether the military could rely entirely on a privately owned merchant marine.

> Senator Magnuson. You feel that the Navy must continue to operate a certain portion of military merchant marine.
> Admiral Callaghan. I do, definitely.
> Senator Magnuson. How long would you say that should continue?
> Admiral Callaghan. I should say that would continue until the world situation approximated that perhaps in the early twenties or early thirties before the threat of a second world war faced us.[35]

In a period of tight DOD budgets, Admiral Callaghan's position may have become an unaffordable luxury. A choice may have to be made between additional B-1 bombers and Trident submarines *or* maintaining a MAC, MTMC, and MSC in their present form. The same choice may have to be made about naval shipyards. If significant savings can be made by placing all naval overhaul and repair work in private yards, can the country afford to do otherwise?

---

[35] U.S. Congress, Senate, Subcommittee of the Committee on Interstate and Foreign Commerce, *Hearings, Merchant Marine Study and Investigation (Transportation of Cargoes by the Military)*, 81st Cong., 2d sess., March 1950, p. 1071. Admiral Callaghan's testimony covered a wide range of topics, including a quite negative comment on the British use of merchant ships in an underway replenishment role during World War II. A reading of the entire hearings is recommended to those interested in early MSTS policy on use of privately owned merchant ships to move military cargo.

The answer, however, is not that clear-cut. The 1973 Arab-Israeli War made an important point—in a quick and dirty situation, an almost instant transportation response is necessary. Can civilian transportation be made that *responsive?* That question and others will be addressed in the remaining chapters of this study.

3

THE MERCHANT MARINE
AS A NAVAL AUXILIARY

Every major twentieth-century maritime enactment has recited the intent of Congress about the role of the merchant marine as a naval and military auxiliary. The Shipping Act of 1916 called for the creation of a naval auxiliary and naval reserve. The Merchant Marine Acts of 1920 and 1928 called for the acquisition of suitable vessels. The Merchant Marine Act of 1936 reaffirmed the declared purposes of the earlier acts and precisely outlined how the "auxiliary" role was to be accomplished. And the Merchant Marine Act of 1970— the last major maritime legislation—ordered 300 vessels to be constructed in 1971–80 to support previous legislation.

This chapter considers to what extent the naval auxiliary objectives set forth in the above legislation have been met. Additional programs and policies intended to enhance the value of the merchant marine in war and in national emergencies are also reviewed.

The 1936 Act and Later Amendments

Naval auxiliary provisions of the 1936 act as amended are summarized below:

Section 210. Merchant ships shall be designed to be quickly convertible into transport and supply vessels in a national emergency. The Maritime Commission—and its successor, the Maritime Administration—is to cooperate closely with the Navy Department.

Section 301 (g). All deck and engineer officers employed on vessels receiving an operating-differential subsidy shall, if eligible, be members of the U.S. Naval Reserve.

Section 501 (b). Plans and specifications for vessels built with a construction-differential subsidy shall be submitted to the Navy Department for approval with respect to the vessel's quick and economical convertibility to a naval or military auxiliary.[1]

Section 502 (b). Any additional cost incurred by incorporating national defense features into a vessel's design shall be paid for by the government.

Section 602 (b). Any additional vessel operating costs incurred because of inclusion of national defense features in the vessel design will be included in the operating differential subsidy.

Section 216 (a), dated June 23, 1938. The Maritime Administration is to provide for training of U.S. citizens to serve as licensed personnel on merchant ships and to establish a voluntary uniformed service for the merchant marine—the U.S. Maritime Service. (The U.S. Merchant Marine Cadet Corps was established in 1938, and the U.S. Merchant Marine Academy in 1943.)

Maritime Academy Act of 1958. This legislation provides financial assistance for states and territories that operate maritime academies or colleges. It supports goals enumerated in Section 101 of the Merchant Marine Act of 1936.

Section 210, dated October 21, 1970. The Maritime Administration is to be responsible for the creation and maintenance of an efficient shipbuilding and repair capacity in the United States with sufficient numbers of skilled personnel to provide an adequate mobilization base.

Merchant Marine Naval Reserve Program

There are basically two ways to qualify for a commission in the Merchant Marine Naval Reserve (MMNR). The traditional method requires, after a high school education, working through unlicensed shipboard positions and taking a standard government examination for licensing as a merchant marine officer. If otherwise eligible, the new merchant marine officer may then apply for a naval reserve commission. Depending upon employment opportunities, this option can take from seven to ten years or longer. Experience and the marketplace are dominant factors in this method of officer procurement. The alternative is to attend a four-year state maritime academy or the four-year federal merchant marine academy at Kings Point, New

---

[1] This was also a requirement under the Merchant Marine Act of 1928, Section 405 (a).

York. After completing the prescribed course of instruction, graduates sit for their original licenses as third mates or third assistant engineers. If the licenses are issued and they are otherwise eligible, these new officers may also apply for a commission. As a condition of acceptance, graduates of federally assisted state maritime schools or the federal maritime academy must accept a naval reserve commission if it is offered.

Development of the Reserve Program. Although the Shipping Act of 1916 called for a merchant marine naval reserve, it was not until passage of the 1936 act that the concept received serious attention. The Merchant Marine Act of 1928 had provided for naval officers on the active list to sail aboard merchant vessels holding government mail contracts and receive half pay from the government. The intent of this provision, however, was not to further a merchant marine naval reserve.

Prior to World War II, the vast majority of merchant marine officers came up through the ranks, but a growing number graduated from the state maritime schools or training ships. The Merchant Marine Act of 1936 intended this latter group to be the nucleus of a merchant marine naval reserve. Merchant marine reserve officers were given the designator 1108—a designator used exclusively for the merchant marine. A vessel with the prescribed number of naval reserve officers aboard was eligible to fly the naval reserve flag. In 1952, however, the special merchant marine designator was abolished, and merchant marine naval reserve officers became surface line officers with the general 1105 designator. During the next decade, perhaps because of the loss of the designator, general lack of interest, or union hostility, the merchant marine naval reserve program declined, and in 1962 it was discontinued.

In response to some concern in Congress, the MMNR program was reestablished in May 1973. Good rapport had developed between the maritime administrator and the chief of naval operations, and this, in turn, contributed to a revived awareness in the navy that the merchant marine indeed had a vital role to play in defense transportation. The MMNR program was opened on a voluntary basis to all deck, engine, and radio officers. The program focused on the merchant marine detachment, a unit composed of officers serving aboard merchant vessels who would have the responsibility for the multibillion dollar U.S. merchant marine performing as a naval auxiliary in time of war or national emergency.

Training for merchant marine naval reserve officers is accomplished primarily through correspondence courses. Active duty training is an option, but funds budgeted for officer pay are limited. In fiscal year 1974, the navy requested $1,962,000 for funding *all* naval reserve component personnel, an amount calculated to support an average selected reserve strength of 116,981.[2] Although the MMNR program had been reestablished in May 1973, Vice Admiral D. W. Cooper, chief of naval reserve affairs, failed to mention it in his October 9, 1973, testimony before a subcommittee of the House Appropriations Committee. His description of the Naval Reserve Military Sealift Command program, however, did appear in the record:

> The Naval Reserve Military Sealift Command program provides a trained manpower surge capability to meet the initial mobilization requirements required by the Military Sealift Command. This surge capability meets the MSC objective to further MSC ability to provide effective and economical sealift transportation for the military departments of the Department of Defense in times of national emergency or war.[3]

Testimony in 1974 and 1975 also omitted mention of the MMNR program.[4]

The Military Sealift Command has the task of promoting the MMNR program. Administrative responsibility is assigned to the district commandants under the chief of naval reserve affairs. Under MSC auspices, the first reserve unit was established in May 1974. Growth since then has reportedly been slow. Although no figures have been published, probably fewer than 100 merchant marine officers serving on privately operated ships have been commissioned, and probably less than $100,000 has been spent directly on the MMNR effort since its inception. The Maritime Administration supports the MMNR through its regional offices, primarily by disseminating information about the program.

Federal Support for Maritime Education. Recent federal funding of maritime officer education—an indirect support for the merchant marine naval reserve—is shown in Table 2.

---

[2] U.S. Congress, House, Subcommittee, Committee on Appropriations, *Department of Defense Appropriations for 1974, Part 10,* 93d Cong., 1st sess., October 1973, p. 134.

[3] House, Subcommittee of Committee on Appropriations, *Hearings on Defense Appropriations 1974,* p. 169.

[4] The FY 1976 naval reserve request was for $164.8 million to support a selected reserve component of 93,972 men. See U.S. Congress, House, Subcommittee of Committee on Appropriations, *Hearings on Department of Defense Appropriations for 1976, Part 6,* 94th Cong., 1st sess., October 1975, pp. 235–236.

Table 2

PROPOSED FEDERAL EXPENDITURES FOR MARITIME EDUCATION, FISCAL YEARS 1976–77

	FY 1976	FY 1977
Kings Point	$11,500,000	$12,301,000
State maritime academies[a]	$ 5,808,000	$ 3,658,000

[a] States with maritime academies are California, Michigan, New York, Maine, Massachusetts, and Texas.
Source: Maritime Authorization—Fiscal Year 1976 *Report No. 94-175*, House of Representatives, 94th Cong., 1st sess.

In 1974, a total of 657 new merchant marine officer licenses, exclusive of those for radio officers, were issued: 182 were graduated from Kings Point, 370 came from the state schools, and 105 came from the engine room or off the deck. Many of those in the last category completed union school courses or privately sponsored refresher courses before sitting for their examinations.[5]

Over the years, as employment opportunities at sea have varied, debate on the federal government's role in maritime officer education has waxed and waned. In time of national emergency—with no problem of employment for merchant marine officers—criticism of the federal effort diminishes. With large numbers of officers looking for jobs, criticism mounts.

Debate over the role of the state academies in relation to the federal academy also emerges periodically. Supporters of state maritime academies have argued that maritime officer education was mainly an obligation of the states but with federal support. They stressed that shipping was a private industry and training of merchant marine personnel should therefore be under state supervision. Speaking before a panel on education and training in a 1954 American merchant marine conference, Admiral C. T. Durgin said:

> I am not here to argue that we do not need a federal maritime college. I do say we first should exhaust the states,

---

[5] U.S. Department of Commerce, *Annual Report of the Maritime Administration for FY 1974*, p. 39. Examples of privately sponsored courses are the Calhoun Engineering School in Baltimore, Md., operated by the Marine Engineers Beneficial Association, and the Merchant Marine School in New York City, operated by the Seaman's Church Institute of New York.

and get all the training we can, or all the aid we can from the states, because that is a state job rather than a federal job.[6]

And speaking earlier before the same group, Rear Admiral H. J. Tiedemann, chief, Office of Maritime Training, said:

> The question has often been asked as to why there is a need for a General Maritime Training Program and if so, what does it accomplish? In considering this question we first must realize that ocean shipping and foreign travel are in the nature of public utilities and of vital importance to our national economy. . . . National defense demands a strong merchant marine. . . . Every major country in the family of nations, and most of the smaller ones, provide education facilities, in whole or in part, at government expense, for their merchant seamen.[7]

Maritime unions usually contend that new officers coming up through the unlicensed ranks can supply the needed numbers both in peace and in time of national emergency. They point to Maritime Administration statistics showing that between June 30, 1967, and June 30, 1968, the height of the Vietnam buildup, a total of 250 deck and engine officers graduated from the training programs of the seafaring unions. This number was approximately one-third of the total of new officers produced in that year. Kings Point graduated 179, and the state academies 342.[8]

As American involvement in Vietnam ended in the early 1970s and ships were returned to the National Defense Reserve Fleet, the question of maritime education arose again—What were to be the roles of the U.S. Merchant Marine Academy, the state academies, and the union training programs? Each had its supporters, and each was prepared to argue its case. Newer and more technologically complex ships, it was claimed, would require merchant marine officers, especially marine engineers, of superior intellect, skill, and training. Could officers coming out of union schools or obtaining their licenses through private study handle such ships as well as those from the state academies and the merchant marine academy at Kings Point?[9]

---

[6] C. T. Durgin, "Labor-Management Policy and the Maritime College Graduate," *Proceedings of American Merchant Marine Conference*, vol. 20 (December 1954), p. 68.

[7] H. J. Tiedemann, "Training of Merchant Marine Officers and Seamen," *Proceedings of American Merchant Marine Conference*, vol. 18 (October 1952), p. 248.

[8] U.S. Department of Commerce, *Annual Report of the Maritime Administration FY 1968*, pp. 50–51.

[9] Joseph Locetta, "Manpower and the Merchant Marine," *U.S. Naval Institute Proceedings*, vol. 96 (July 1970), p. 29.

Questions also arose over the financial difficulties faced by the state academies, with decreasing federal support and increasing costs.[10]

In May 1974 the Office of Maritime Manpower of the Maritime Administration released its third report in a series on manpower planning. While the earlier reports did not forecast officer shortages, the 1974 study did allow for such a possibility by 1979–80.[11] The Maritime Administration report made three recommendations.[12] (1) Ways should be found to increase the retention of graduates of federal and state academies in seafaring careers. (2) New officers should come initially from industry schools such as the Calhoun Engineering School in Baltimore, Maryland. (3) Increased federal support of state schools should be considered.

The first recommendation is of the most interest since it points up a fact long known in the maritime industry, that is, significant numbers of maritime academy graduates, state and federal, are not employed as merchant marine officers.[13] Some may work in marine-related fields, but this is not the intended result of federal funding for maritime education. Federal support cannot be justified for a certain number of new officers to be graduated each year if many of the graduates become employed ashore. In the future, federal maritime education expenditures will probably be sought to provide training for shoreside positions in the shipping industry and in marine-related fields, such as naval architecture and marine and ocean engineering.

MMNR Summary and Evaluation. The intent of Congress to establish an effective merchant marine naval reserve has been only partially realized. On the one hand, the concept has not had the unqualified support of the navy. On the other hand, a great deal of federal money has been funneled into maritime officer training, creating a surplus of officers who can find employment only in shoreside positions.

In 1975, there were three sources of new merchant marine officers: the federally operated academy at Kings Point, the six state maritime academies, and the privately operated refresher courses and union schools for unlicensed seamen. In peacetime the output of officers from these sources is likely to exceed available berths at sea.

---

[10] William B. Hayler, "Our Imperiled State Maritime Academies," *U.S. Naval Institute Proceedings*, vol. 98 (June 1972), p. 57.

[11] U.S. Department of Commerce, Office of Maritime Manpower, *Deck and Engine Officers in the U.S. Merchant Marine: Supply and Demand 1974–1984* (Washington, D.C.: Maritime Administration, 1974), pp. 3–4.

[12] Ibid., pp. 5–6.

[13] National Research Council, *Research and Education for Maritime Progress* (Washington, D.C.: National Academy of Sciences, January 1973), p. 36.

In a prolonged mobilization or contingency, however, any surplus of officers will probably be absorbed in an expanded merchant marine.

A well-conceived and well-supported ready reserve composed primarily of federal and state maritime academy graduates employed ashore could provide the additional officers needed in an emergency. The program could follow the navy's present ready reserve in concept and scope. The shore-based reservist would be expected to maintain his proficiency in a prescribed training program, including periodic three-week coastwise voyages of two or three weeks. Such training would give the coast guard sufficient reason to issue a waiver if his license expired (as it has to officers returning to sea from shoreside employment in past contingency situations, such as Vietnam). This strategy would provide a supply of officers at sea in a contingency or mobilization situation. Such a program would relieve pressure for greater federal expenditures for merchant marine officer education. It would, however, require a navy dedication to an effective merchant marine naval reserve program, in terms of both manpower and funding.

It is doubtful, particularly in the present economic environment, that state academies can continue without a substantial increase in federal support. This possibility raises the question of whether it would not be more cost-effective to close Kings Point and train merchant marine officers at state schools.[14] Serious consideration was given to this alternative in 1954. The union schools and the privately sponsored refresher courses for seamen seeking officer licenses also pose questions. Should the states and the federal government encourage their expansion? These two sources—particularly the union schools—have given little more than lukewarm support to the concept of a merchant marine naval reserve. Those seeking to cut defense-related expenditures without impairing sealift readiness may well ask why, as well as demand answers to other questions related to maritime education.

Merchant Ship National Defense Features

The previous chapter discussed the effectiveness of the civilian-manned merchant ship in its role as a privateer. Typically, with the beginning of hostilities, civilian ships were fitted out as this type of naval auxiliary, but, as privateering became more lucrative, ships were

---

[14] Hayler, *U.S. Naval Institute Proceedings*, p. 53. Hayler estimates that the cost to the federal government for a state academy graduate is $5,000, compared with $19,000 for his Kings Point counterpart.

often built with a number of defensive and offensive features, such as hulls designed for greater speed, extra sail, and gun ports.

Use of merchant ships in an offensive manner, that is, privateering, was prohibited by an agreement among the maritime powers in 1856. The United States was not a signatory, an omission it was later to regret when armed Confederate raiders put to sea in 1862. These raiders were, in fact, naval vessels, but for purposes of public opinion in the North were classified as privateers—a classification that was not accepted by the major European powers.

During World War I, German and British merchant ships were fitted out as commerce raiders and U-boat decoys. They were manned, however, by naval personnel. Since World War II, the merchant ship has performed more as a true auxiliary, providing logistical support to naval and military forces. In this role, the vessel is equipped for combat contingencies, but does not seek combat.

National Defense Features in the Nuclear Age. Authority for incorporating national defense features into new merchant ship construction is found in Title V of the Merchant Marine Act of 1936, as amended. Section 501 (b) requires that plans of vessels built with a construction differential subsidy be submitted to the navy for approval. Section 502 (b) makes the government responsible for any additional cost of national defense features, and Section 602 (b) of Title VI provides that any additional operating costs incurred by incorporating national defense features in vessel design be included in the operating differential subsidy.[15] Some desirable national defense features on a merchant ship include: (1) a minimum sustained speed of twenty knots; (2) sufficient compartmentation to survive in case of damage; (3) redundancy of certain equipment, such as extra generators (or space left to install them later), fire-fighting equipment (including aircraft fire-fighting capability if a helicopter pad is an included national defense feature), extra fresh-water evaporators, extra washdown equipment in the event of nuclear, biological, or chemical exposure; (4) stowage spaces designed to accommodate outsize military equipment; (5) heavy lift gear and a self-sustaining discharge capability; (6) UHF radiotelephone equipment, capable of establishing communications with naval vessels; (7) in tankers, capabilities for fast pumping and for underway replenishment of navy vessels; (8)

---

[15] Plans for vessels built with a construction differential subsidy are submitted to the assistant secretary of the navy (installations and logistics) for approval. A good summary of national defense features is found in U.S. Congress, House, Seapower Subcommittee of Committee on Armed Services, *Hearings on Current Status of Shipyards 1974*, 93d Cong., 2d sess., October 1974, pp. 1240–1243.

also in tankers, capability to carry multiple wet cargoes, such as different fuels.

Defense Versus Commercial Requirements. Although few disagree with the concept of incorporating national defense features into new vessel construction, conflicts arise in practice between military and commercial requirements. Consider vessel speed, for example. From a defense point of view, the greater the speed the better, but from a commercial viewpoint, the advantages of greater speed must be balanced against additional construction costs, efficiency in operation, and the competitive demands of trade (that is, if fast service is not a trade requirement, putting a thirty-three knot ship on that trade is hardly economical). Similar questions could be asked about other defense features. Is it economically rational, for example, to require a self-sustaining discharge capability on board a non-self-sustaining containership?

Although the Merchant Marine Act of 1936 provides for the additional costs of national defense features to be paid by the government, several vexing questions arise over implementation of the act:

(1) Not all American vessels are built under the act, that is, with a construction differential subsidy. Much recent tanker construction falls into this category.

(2) The amount of money available for national defense features is limited, and it is included in the total construction differential subsidy funds. If nineteen vessels are fitted with national defense features, for example, funds for the construction of a twentieth vessel may not be available, depending upon the total subsidy funds appropriated. There may be a trade-off between the number of ships built with these funds and the number of ships equipped with national defense features. In its role as promoter of the merchant marine in toto, the Maritime Administration must favor a greater number of ships rather than a smaller number equipped with national defense features. The present method of funding national defense features almost precludes a new ship leaving the yard optimally equipped with national defense features. At present national defense feature funds, as a part of construction differential subsidy funds, are controlled by the Maritime Administration, which would probably oppose a navy takeover of the national defense feature program even if the navy were willing to invest more money.

(3) The suitability of a vessel for economical and speedy conversion into a naval or military auxiliary in time of war or national emergency raises serious questions. The navy may review the plans

for a ship, decide it has no national defense use, and recommend no national defense features. In this case the Maritime Administration may either approve the construction differential subsidy application regardless, or negotiate with the shipowner to make the vessel more suitable, or disapprove the contract. The vessel as proposed, however, may well be in the best commercial interest of the United States.[16] The problem can be compounded if facilities and materials are in short supply, as shipyards and steel were in 1974, and if a building priority is required under the Defense Production Act of 1950. If construction of the "unsuitable" ship is thereby delayed or cancelled, the Maritime Administration—charged by law with promoting the entire merchant marine—may well dispute the navy's verdict. Such disagreements have occurred in the past and will again in the future. The Maritime Administration's attempt to gain a material priority for the construction of liquid natural gas carriers and ultra-large crude carriers is a recent example.[17]

Expenditures on National Defense Features, 1958–74. A Maritime Administration statistical summary published in January 1975 stated that, on the 240 ships constructed since 1958 for a total contract price of $5.4 billion, only $14.6 million—or about 0.27 percent of the total —had been spent for national defense features. Five vessels had no national defense features whatever. Between 1955 and 1974, 67 ships were converted at a cost of $315 million, but national defense features were on only four ships for a total cost of $52,800.[18] Reasonable men may disagree whether a particular ship warrants a national defense feature expenditure, but they could only conclude that these features are being installed less often than Congress intended in the 1936 act. Points worthy of consideration on this problem include the following:

(1) Funds for national defense features could be made a line item in the Maritime Administration budget, that is, a specific amount could be appropriated for this purpose. If nothing else, congressional oversight would be simplified.

---

[16] One Maritime Administration official has suggested that certain basic national defense features be incorporated into all vessels built with construction differential subsidy funds at government expense. When the shipowner uses the national defense feature in his commercial operations, the government would be reimbursed. When the 20-knot Mariner class dry cargo ships were built on government account in the early 1950s, most industry spokesmen considered such a speed uneconomical. In time, however, the 20-knot speed was recognized as a commercial asset.

[17] "The Supertanker Steel Squeeze," *Business Week*, May 18, 1974, pp. 28–29.

[18] U.S. Maritime Administration, Division of Costs and Estimates, *Title V New Construction Contracts Merchant Marine Act, 1936 as Amended* (January 1975).

(2) Funding of national defense features could be transferred to the navy and made a line item in the navy budget.

(3) Funds could be appropriated as a line item in the Maritime Administration budget to compensate a vessel owner for operating losses incurred because of incorporating national defense features on this ship. Payment would be decided on a ship-by-ship basis and would be independent of money appropriated for operating differential subsidies.

(4) To encourage the fitting of defense features on American-flag vessels, whether built with a construction differential subsidy or not, the Military Sealift Command in contracting for DOD cargoes could give preference to vessels capable of serving as a military and naval auxiliary. National defense suitability could be made a specific requirement for receiving Title XI federal ship mortgage insurance.

(5) The assistant secretary of the navy (installations and logistics) could be required to publish specific guidelines defining suitability for defense purposes. Every vessel would be assumed to have some minimum national defense value. The initial draft of the guidelines would be made available to the Maritime Administration, Congress, the armed services, shipbuilders, and ship operators for comment, and the final document would reflect their input and judgments. An a priori understanding of what constitutes suitability for national defense would mitigate disputes about a vessel's priority under the Defense Production Act of 1950.

Defense Equipping of Merchant Ships. Somewhat akin to the national defense feature concept is the defensive equipping of merchant ships. Incorporating national defense features into a ship is a passive measure, but defensive-equipping is an active one. Strengthening decks to accommodate army tanks, for example, is a very desirable national defense feature, but mounting guns and assigning gun crews, as was done in World War II, is a more affirmative action.

Concern about protecting merchant shipping in a period of hostilities has become more pronounced in the 1970s. The following comments reflect this concern.

> Economically, containerization is a golden goose; militarily, it could become an albatross. Consider this: In World War II, the number of enemy submarines was small and the number of Allied ships was extremely large. In a future war, the U.S.S.R. could put to sea ten times as many commerce raiders as Hitler managed, against perhaps a tenth as many ships.[19]

---

[19] Frank B. Case, "The Versatile, Vulnerable Containership," *U.S. Naval Institute Proceedings*, vol. 98 (February 1972), p. 48.

A containership which provides the sustained lift capacity of four or five conventional freighters, when sunk, represents the loss of four or five conventional freighter equivalents. The value of enemy torpedoes has been multiplied by the same economics which have promoted modernization of the U.S. merchant marine.[20]

A supertanker can be so large that one of them equals an entire World War II convoy in carrying capacity. Their size requires considerable sea room for almost every evolution. Could convoy doctrine of World War II be successfully applied to them: Probably not.[21]

U.S. and other NATO naval forces combined couldn't get our military shipping safely across the Atlantic (let alone bring in essential oil) against submarine opposition.[22]

Among the possibilities for defense equipping, one that has attracted considerable congressional interest is the ARAPAHO program. In this program, at least six helicopters, with maintenance facilities, would be placed aboard large, fast containerships, in order to give the merchant ship an independent anti-submarine-warfare capability.[23]

Today the national defense features and defense equipping of merchant ships programs are administered by different agencies, though there are channels for coordination. The question remains, however, whether an *upgraded* national defense feature program can be administered independently of a defense equipping of merchant ships program when, at some point, the two concepts seem to converge. Providing for a helicopter pad and supporting personnel in a ship's plan, for example, would probably be considered a national defense feature, and so would provision for a helicopter repair capability in the ship's machine shop. Stowing aboard six or more disassembled helicopters, however, is an implementation of defense equipping of merchant ships. Both programs should be considered together. Responsibility for the defense equipping of merchant ships

---

[20] Frank B. Case, "Time to Secure the Seas," *U.S. Naval Institute Proceedings*, vol. 99 (August 1973), p. 27.

[21] J. W. Aber, Jr. and Paul W. Garber, "The Navy and Merchant Marine: A Critical Coalition," *U.S. Naval Institute Proceedings*, vol. 96 (March 1970), p. 43.

[22] Case, "Time to Secure the Seas," p. 26.

[23] J. V. Jollif and G. D. Kerr, "Designing for Change: Present and Future," *U.S. Naval Institute Proceedings*, vol. 100 (July 1974), pp. 33–34. In October 1975 the navy awarded a $5,330,000 contract to design, build, and demonstrate a prototype of the system. At the urging of Representative George H. Mahon, Chairman of the House Committee on Appropriations, the system, now named the Reserve Merchant Ship Defense System, will be manned by naval reservists.

is with the Naval Systems Command, Office of Maritime Affairs, in DOD, and for national defense features with the Maritime Administration, in the Department of Commerce. At a minimum a permanent joint committee should be established and supported by the Maritime Administration and the navy. Navy support, particularly in regard to manpower, is essential, as is a good informal working relationship between the navy, the Maritime Administration, shipbuilders, and the shipping industry—including the maritime unions. If the concerns cited above have any merit at all, protection of the merchant marine naval auxiliary deserves a high priority in DOD mobilization planning.

Underway Replenishment of Naval Forces

Underway replenishment of naval warships is a task as old as navies themselves. The United States maintains four active fleets. The Third Fleet, headquartered at Pearl Harbor, operates in the 50 million square miles of the eastern Pacific and the mid-Pacific. The Seventh Fleet operates in the western Pacific, the Second Fleet is responsible for the eastern Atlantic, and the Sixth Fleet patrols the Mediterranean. The importance of replenishing these fleets is somewhat more obvious than the amount of shipping required for the task. Traditionally, this mission has required a substantial part of the navy budget.

Underway replenishment to an on-station fleet involves the carriage of both wet and dry cargo. A resupply ship may replenish fleet vessels directly or in a consolidation mode, that is, by transferring its cargo, after making the long leg of the journey, to an auxiliary assigned to the fleet. For example, a consolidation tanker may load at Los Angeles and discharge in the western Pacific to one or more Seventh Fleet tankers.

Background. The navy has built, manned, and maintained its own fleet of underway replenishment ships, usually armed. *Jane's Fighting Ships 1974–75* lists U.S. Navy types as oilers (AO), ammunition ships (AE), stores ships (AF), combat stores ship (AFS), stores issue ships (AKS), combat support ships (AOE), gasoline tankers (AOG), replenishment oilers (AOR), auxiliary tugs (ATA), fleet tugs (ATF), and salvage tugs (ATS). A total of 103 ships are listed in the above classes.[24]

---

[24] John E. Moore, ed., *Jane's Fighting Ships 1974–75* (New York: Franklin Watts, 1974).

Another navy fleet in the general merchant-type category is operated by the Military Sealift Command. This fleet supports not only navy installations overseas but also the army and air force as well. In this "sealift" category, *Jane's* lists cargo ships (AK), vehicle cargo ships (AKR), tankers (AO), gasoline tankers (AOG), and LST type vessels. Additionally, MSC operates a number of special purpose ships, such as cable repair ships (ARC) and hydrographic vessels. These vessels are not armed, and most are manned by American civil service personnel. At the end of FY 1974, MSC was operating 96 of these government-owned ships and had 69 vessels on charter.[25] After the American withdrawal from Vietnam, however, this fleet was reduced to 115 ships in 1975.

In FY 1972, the navy initiated a program to turn over operation of a number of its underway replenishment ships to MSC. Under MSC operation these ships are civil service manned and have on board a military communications detachment.[26] The purpose of the move was to save money. In testimony on the FY 1974 budget, Secretary of the Navy John Warner estimated annual savings as $760,000 for fleet oilers, $820,000 for fleet ocean tugs, and $1,700,000 for store ships.[27]

Initially the transfer was limited to oilers, tugs, and store ships, plus navy-manned cable-repair ships. The program of identifying navy underway replenishment missions that could be taken over by MSC is continuing. Combat stores ships are an additional possibility for transfer.

From the navy's point of view, shifting some underway replenishment responsibility to MSC is a trade-off between dollar savings and combat readiness. With the navy budget under increasing pressure, dollar savings have been favored. Navy officials, however, do not intend to shift the entire mission to MSC. In fact, many senior naval officers are concerned about the number of transfers that have already taken place. They fear that savings obtained at the sacrifice of combat efficiency may prove to be a false economy in the long run, particularly in a wartime environment.

Privately Operated Merchant Ships in Underway Replenishment. The navy's willingness to transfer a part of its mission to MSC resulted partly from a joint U.S. Navy-Maritime Administration test. For this

---

[25] Riley, "DOD Transportation: Management Problems," p. 2.

[26] U.S. Department of Defense, *Annual Defense Department Report FY 1976*, p. III-95.

[27] U.S. Congress, Senate, Committee on Appropriations, *Hearings, Department of Defense Appropriations FY 1974, Part 3*, 93d Cong., 1st sess., p. 41.

test, a typical union-manned privately owned tanker was modified for an underway replenishment role at a cost of about $30,000. Between February 7 and April 4, 1972, the 35,000-ton U.S.-flag merchant tanker, S.S. *Erna Elizabeth*, operated with navy and NATO vessels in the Atlantic, Mediterranean, and Caribbean. It steamed approximately 13,000 miles and provided underway refueling to some forty navy ships, including the carrier *John F. Kennedy*.[28] Test results were excellent, and all commitments were made on time without sustaining ship damage or incurring a single personnel injury. At the conclusion of the test, Admiral E. R. Zumwalt, Jr., chief of naval operations praised the resourcefulness and initiative of the *Erna Elizabeth* crew:

> It proved the feasibility of using commercial tankers to consolidate Navy replenishment ships and to provide limited replenishment of combatant ships. The knowledge that this surge capability is available can expand the employment options of our Fleet.[29]

A later test, in December 1972, demonstrated the feasibility of using scheduled berth liners to underway-replenish on-station naval vessels with dry stores. A scheduled Lighter Aboard Ship (LASH) vessel, the S.S. *Lash Italia* of Prudential Lines, delivered a token load to an on-station fleet stores ship of the Sixth Fleet. After the lighters were dropped off, the *Lash Italia* continued to its normal ports of call in the Mediterranean. The navy considered this test a success as well. By 1975, the navy had transferred much of its underway replenishment responsibility to MSC, but, apart from the two tests cited above, no privately controlled ship had participated directly in an underway replenishment mission. Indirectly, privately owned vessels have participated insofar as MSC has used chartered commercial tankers in its controlled fleet for consolidation movements.

Since 1972, in testimony before Congress, navy and MSC spokesmen have cited the significant savings being realized by MSC in its new underway replenishment role, but they have said little about the possibility of extending the concept to the privately operated merchant ship.[30] This omission has not gone unnoticed in the industry. Maritime spokesmen point out that equal or greater savings can be

---

[28] U.S. Department of Commerce, *Annual Report of the Maritime Administration 1972*, p. 15.

[29] Ibid.

[30] In the *Annual Defense Department Report FY 1976*, Secretary Schlesinger left the door ajar when he said, "In light of the cost and manpower savings associated with MSC-operated UNREP [underway replenishment] ships, efforts are continuing to identify UNREP missions which MSC operated vessels and *possibly* [italics supplied] commercial ships can carry out." (p. III-96)

realized by using private ships. One point often made is that, though MSC crews are significantly smaller than navy crews on similar ships, wages would amount to even less for union crews. MSC maintains a "pipeline reserve" that effectively adds about 20 percent to the crew payroll, but the pipeline reserve for a union-crewed ship are the seamen registered for jobs at seaport union halls. No charge accrues to vessel-operating cost for maintaining this pool of labor.[31]

In 1975, with a turndown in economic activity and a rising surplus of tonnage on the world tanker markets, the AFL-CIO Maritime Trades Department released a statement about merchant tankers in underway replenishment roles, part of which said:

> One of the largest single areas of the military budget is the $15.4 billion allotted to the construction of Navy vessels. While much of this is for warships to modernize an over age and decimated U.S. Navy combat fleet, some $300 million will go to the Navy's continued efforts to build up its fleet of non-combat support and supply vessels.
>
> The AFL-CIO Maritime Trades Department strongly supports the maintenance of a powerful U.S. Navy. Nevertheless, we oppose the waste of scarce Navy budget funds for support vessels which are readily available in the U.S. private merchant fleet. While in some cases these vessels may require minor modifications to meet the Navy's requirements, they generally are able to be operated at less cost under private management than when operated by the Navy.
>
> The Fiscal Year 1976 budget contains funds for at least several new fleet oilers at a cost of $81 million each, plus two additional ocean tugs. The jobs which these vessels will perform can be handled by privately owned U.S. flag vessels at less cost to the U.S. taxpayer. The fleet oiler in particular will deny potential work to the private U.S. fleet at a time when fully 25 percent of the independent U.S. tanker fleet is unemployed.[32]

The president of the American Waterways Operators, Inc., wrote similar comments in a letter to the secretary of the navy:

> While we certainly appreciate recent initiatives by the Navy to look at its tug situation in a more objective, less

---

[31] This would depend somewhat on crew turnover and union policy. Usually a man leaving a ship and the new man both receive a day's pay. Another consideration is the cost to the private company for contributions to union pension funds, as contrasted with the ultimate cost to the government of a retired civil servant.

[32] *Position on Appropriations: Statement Adopted by the AFL-CIO Maritime Trades Department Executive Board*, Bal Harbour, Florida, February 13–14, 1975.

protective manner, we feel additional initiatives are due. We commend the Navy for hiring outside research organizations to examine tug needs. We are confident that such studies will show the Navy tugboat program to be inefficient and wasteful of money and manpower.

The letter went on to point out that the navy had an estimated 142 tugboats operating in the continental United States, Hawaii, Guam, and Puerto Rico, where excellent commercial service is available. The letter concluded:

In this era of budget restraint, steps must be taken to insure that the limited dollars available for national defense and in particular for the Naval Service are not wasted on activities which could easily be handled by the private sector of the economy.[33]

The navy and MSC have cited a number of objections to the use of privately operated, union-manned vessels for peacetime underway replenishment missions: (1) Merchant ships are subject to delays caused by crew work stoppages. (2) Merchant officers and seamen do not have the necessary security clearance. (3) Merchant ships lack the required communications equipment (and communications staff) to communicate effectively with naval vessels. (4) Merchant seamen typically do not have the necessary skills to perform the underway replenishment mission efficiently. (5) Merchant tankers must be modified structurally to perform the necessary tasks. (6) In hostilities, danger to merchant crews is a consideration.

For the moment the navy has gone about as far as it intends with respect to transferring its underway replenishment mission to MSC. As stated by Secretary of the Navy John Warner in 1974:

It would be neither feasible nor practical to operate combatant or many types of support ships with civilian crews. One obvious reason is that the military skills needed to man a combatant ship, as well as the highly trained technicians to support these ships from our tenders and repair ships, do not exist in the U.S. civilian labor force. Therefore, I do not envision the program expanding to encompass other ship types that have already been or are planned for turnover to

---

[33] Letter to Honorable J. William Middendorf, secretary of the navy from James R. Smith, president, American Waterways Operators, Inc., dated February 20, 1975. A recent study determined that, in fact, "Greater reliance on the commercial sector for tugboat services with a concurrent deactivation of Navy tugboats could bring about significant savings to the Department of Defense." See Comptroller General of the U.S., *Letter Report B-133170* (Washington, D.C.: U.S. General Accounting Office, 1975), p. 1.

MSC, via oilers (AO), cable repair ships (ARC), fleet ocean tugs (ATF), and store ships (AF).[34]

If Warner's thesis is accepted, one must ask whether there is also a significant difference between MSC civil-service-operated ships and privately operated ships in a limited underway replenishment role. In this context, points one through six are again considered.

(1) Delay—for any reason—of a ship on an underway replenishment mission is a justified concern, so the possibility of a delay caused by crew strikes cannot be ignored. Would a no-strike agreement between DOD and the unions be effective? There is simply no answer until it is tried. Although the navy cannot be expected to turn over all underway replenishment missions now performed by MSC vessels in a single stroke, it could risk a few ships on a trial basis to learn whether union-manned underway replenishment vessels would sail despite a work stoppage affecting other commercial shipping. The possibility of a work stoppage by underway replenishment crews is a valid concern, but manning ships with civil service personnel is not an ironclad guarantee against vessel delays. The question is, In the present labor environment, would civil service employees agree not to join unions or not to strike?

(2) The question of security clearance for merchant marine officers and seamen requires study and data that are not now available. How many officers and seamen on an underway replenishment vessel require clearance, for example, and at what level? It has been suggested that only the ship's master and radio officer need clearances, and no higher than secret. If, as a precondition for underway replenishment employment, all ship's officers were required to be members of the Merchant Marine Naval Reserve, or, at a minimum, those officers needing a clearance were members, then obtaining clearances for such officers should not be difficult, costly, or time consuming. A merchant officer or seaman may be assumed to possess some level of "clearance" by virtue of his mariner's document or officer's license. To what extent does the investigation required for these papers parallel the National Agency Check, the basic background investigation for a security clearance?

(3) The *Erna Elizabeth* test demonstrated that effective com-

---

[34] U.S. Congress, Senate, Committee on Appropriations, *Hearings, Department of Defense Appropriations FY 1975, Part 3*, 93d Cong., 2d sess., p. 28. The question of civilian vs. navy crews was briefly discussed in National Research Council, *Containership Underway Replenishment: A Study of the Use of Containerships for the Underway Replenishment of Naval Vessels* (Washington, D.C.: National Academy of Sciences, 1971). The panel thought the option of civilian crews deserved consideration. Also, the subsequently cited Merchant Ship Naval Auxiliary Program envisions civilian crews in wartime.

munications between naval and merchant vessels require additional communications equipment aboard merchant ships. Such equipment, however, is not expensive and would seem to qualify as a national defense feature. If not, a shipowner would probably meet this requirement at his own expense if it resulted in the employment of his vessel.

(4) If merchant seamen and officers do not possess underway replenishment skills, those skills can be acquired. The Maritime Administration is required under the amended Merchant Marine Act of 1936, section 216 (a), "to prescribe such courses and periods of training . . . as necessary to maintain a trained and efficient merchant marine personnel." Lacking this, the maritime unions could offer the necessary courses and training.

(5) Some structural modification of existing commercial tankers for an underway replenishment role is required. This was demonstrated in the *Erna Elizabeth* test. The modifications and cost would, of course, depend on the underway replenishment role contemplated. The cost of modification would be borne by the vessel owner, who would have to decide whether vessel earnings in underway replenishment would justify the expense—a marketplace decision. If idle tonnage exists—as was the case with tankers in 1975—a shipowner would probably deem the expense worthwhile. No structural modification was required in the *Lash Italia* dry cargo underway replenishment test using a lighter aboard ship. But other types of dry cargo ships would probably require some modifications, particularly in cargo gear. This also would be a decision in which modification costs would be weighed against potential vessel earnings.

(6) Danger to crews in case of hostile action should present no more or less of a problem than was encountered in World War II, Korea, and Vietnam. It is difficult to see a difference between danger to a civil service crew and danger to a union crew.

The Sealift Readiness Program

Since the end of World War II, the privately owned merchant marine has carried the majority of DOD cargo. In peacetime most of this cargo goes to berth liners. In time of a military buildup, as in the Korean and Vietnam wars, government-owned tonnage increases along with the amount of private shipping chartered by DOD. The berth liners' share, but not necessarily their total tonnage, decreases correspondingly. In FY 1968, during the Vietnam buildup, government-owned shipping carried approximately 36 percent of DOD dry cargo. Six years later, in FY 1974, its share had dropped to less than 10 percent. MSC moved 28 million long tons (of 2,240 pounds each), in FY 1968, and an estimated 15 million in FY 1975.[35] With the complete disengagement of U.S. forces in Vietnam and a general American retrenchment in Southeast Asia, this figure was estimated at 10 million measurement tons (of 40 cubic feet each) for FY 1976 and was expected to level out at that amount thereafter.

Although DOD cargo accounts for only a small percentage of total industry revenue, it can be quite important to a particular company, especially as a source of revenue on a particular route.[36] The private shipping firms' desire to participate in this cargo movement and to earn revenues from defense cargoes is the foundation of Sealift Readiness Program.

When the Military Sealift Command was assigned responsibility for DOD sealift procurement, in 1949, commercial shipping service was procured by space charter. Under this system, the government contracted with individual companies for a specific amount of space on their vessels. Payment was made whether or not the space was used. In 1950, these space charters were converted to "shipping contracts," which were more equitable to the government viewpoint in space use and stevedoring charges. Under a uniform rate structure, cargo was assigned to firms by frequency of sailings on a particular route. Neither space chartering nor its later modification completely satisfied the industry, DOD, and the Federal Maritime Commission, the regulatory agency that approves ocean freight rates.

In 1966, a method of competitive procurement was introduced. Firms thereafter submitted bids on various categories of cargo, the low bidder generally receiving the lion's share. Industry objected to this winner-take-all concept, however, and, after DOD sponsored an interagency study, *Sealift Procurement and National Security (SPANS)* in 1972, the system was modified to limit a low bidder to a maximum of 50 percent of the cargo offered on any one route (in a few cases this figure was increased to 75 percent).[37] In the early 1970s, participation in the Sealift Readiness Program became a prerequisite for bidding on DOD cargo.

---

[35] Sam H. Moore, "Learning How to Manage Sealift Capability," *Defense Management Journal*, vol. 11 (April 1975), p. 28.

[36] U.S. Department of Commerce, Maritime Administration, *Analysis of Requirement for a Cargo Allocation System*, pp. 18–19.

[37] U.S. Department of Defense, *Sealift Procurement and National Security (SPANS)*, Four parts, August 1972. Part I, "Understanding the Current Systems," gives an excellent review of DOD sealift procurement policies since the end of World War II.

Operation of the Program. A continuing problem since the end of World War II has been how to supplement MSC-controlled shipping with commercial shipping when the need arises. Such a need may arise either because of a war, as in Korea and Vietnam, or simply because of an increase in DOD cargo movement, such as increased sales under the Military Assistance Program. As might be expected, in busy periods, shipping space is not always readily available for DOD requirements, while in poor times, participating in defense cargo movement is a matter of survival for many firms—particularly the nonscheduled operators. The Defense Department's basic problem is how to acquire additional sealift in a nonmobilization situation when American-flag shipping is fully employed. With the gradual demise of the tramp sector of U.S.-flag shipping, this problem has become one of acquiring fully employed berth line ships in a nonmobilization contingency. The Department of Defense is constrained from requisitioning privately owned shipping except in a mobilization declared by the President. Any arrangements for taking privately owned ships, therefore, must be voluntary on the part of the shipping firm.

The berth line operator faces a dilemma. If he supports an increased DOD need for shipping, and takes scheduled vessels off their normal trade, in effect cutting back his shipping service, he might lose business to competitors—business he might regain only at considerable expense, if at all.

If the shipping firm decides to bid on DOD cargo, then, to assure that its bid is responsive and will be considered, the company must agree to contract 50 percent of its American-flag fleet to the Sealift Readiness Program, with half to be made available within thirty days and the remainder within sixty days.

The company must also specify the number and type of ships offered, for review by the Maritime Administration and the Office of Emergency Transportation, and it must abide by the following call-up procedure:

(1) The commander of the Military Sealift Command must determine that the shipping is necessary to meet DOD requirements, and that ocean shipping is not available at fair and reasonable rates.

(2) The MSC commander must also determine that shipping available through normal chartering procedures is not suitable.

(3) The secretary of defense must rule that ships of the National Defense Reserve Fleet cannot be responsive either in time or in numbers.

(4) The MSC commander, with the approval of the secretaries

of commerce and defense, must call up the individual ships under the Sealift Readiness Program.

(5) In determining which ships to call up and when, the MSC commander must cooperate with the maritime administrator, who will attempt to equalize the burden among participating carriers.

(6) Vessels offered for charter to MSC subsequent to the call-up will be accepted if in satisfactory condition. Unacceptable ships must be replaced by the operator with an acceptable vessel of equivalent capacity.[38]

As of July 10, 1974, twelve berth line firms had committed a total of 118 ships (57 break-bulk and 61 intermodal) to the Sealift Readiness Program under Request for Proposal 900 (first cycle). This figure is typical of the numbers of ships pledged in the past and expected in the future.

Problems. The Sealift Readiness Program has never been tried: no involuntary call-up of contractually committed ships has ever taken place. When DOD has required additional tonnage, a sufficient number of ships were obtained by chartering and by breaking out ships from the government-owned National Defense Reserve Fleet. Because the Sealift Readiness Program has never been implemented, questions about the program arise, such as the following:

(1) To what extent will firms lose trade—that is, what will be the long-term economic effect—if their vessels are taken off a regularly scheduled service in a Sealift Readiness Program call-up?

(2) Under what conditions might the secretary of commerce veto the call-up of one or more ships? What would be the criteria upon which he would base such a decision?

(3) Does a DOD time charter agreement based primarily on a vessel's operating costs equitably compensate an owner whose vessel is taken? If not, what additional costs does a company incur?

(4) Are the types of ships committed satisfactory to meet a range of contingencies, that is, will MSC obtain the right shipping at the right time?

Other questions have been posed, but these four have caused most

---

[38] Sealift Readiness Agreements are part of all requests for proposals (RFP) put out by the Military Sealift Command in soliciting bids from U.S.-flag steamship companies to move DOD cargo.

concern, particularly in the last two years.[39] In an attempt to answer these questions, the Department of Defense, in cooperation with the Departments of Commerce and Transportation, asked the Maritime Transportation Research Board of the National Academy of Sciences to undertake a study in 1973 to determine the economic effects of call-ups under the Sealift Readiness Program. The final report was published in June 1975. Its major conclusions are summarized below.[40]

(1) As shipping firms have become more capital intensive, they have become more sensitive to fluctuations in revenue, particularly if there is a large investment in equipment not subject to call-up and hence to compensation. This increased vulnerability to revenue fluctuation should be considered when estimating the economic effect of a call-up.

(2) The major factor in judging whether a call-up will benefit or penalize a firm economically is demand for the vessel's services during and after the call-up. A call-up when demand is high could penalize operators if the withdrawn vessels were replaced in their schedules by competitors. On the other hand, if demand is slack, a benefit could accrue to underused vessels. The vessels' return to a static or no-growth market would make their efficient employment difficult and could decrease the firm's share of the market. A growing market, on the other hand, would present fewer reemployment problems.

(3) A call-up of a significant portion of berth line shipping would impact unevenly on the trade routes served by U.S.-flag shipping. Service over heavy volume routes would be least affected, and sailing to low-volume ports and over low-density routes might be curtailed or eliminated entirely.

(4) DOD reliance upon the fleets of berth line operators will be greater than in the past.

(5) Line operators participate in the Sealift Readiness Program in order to be eligible to carry DOD cargo, but they believe that significant costs are omitted in the MSC formula for computing time charter rates.

(6) A firm that commits 50 percent of its ships is not necessarily

---

[39] Questions with respect to the viability of the Sealift Readiness Program have been raised in both the FY 1975 and the FY 1976 annual reports of the Department of Defense. Also, the FY 1976 report of the chairman, joint chiefs of staff, stated "the required vessels could be obtained through commitments made by U.S. flag operators under the SRP [Sealift Readiness Program]. There is considerable concern that these operators would lose some portion of their business to other domestic or foreign lines if their ships were taken off their routes for any substantial period. We are reluctant to use this program."

[40] National Research Council, *The Sealift Readiness Program* (Washington, D.C.: National Academy of Sciences, June 1975), pp. 47–48.

committing 50 percent of its ton-mile capacity. Under Request for Proposal 900 (first cycle), ton-mile capacities ranged from 33 to 72 percent, even though all firms committed one-half the number of vessels in their fleets.

Summary of the Sealift Readiness Program. The National Academy of Sciences study focused needed attention on the Sealift Readiness Program. A viable program, in which DOD has confidence, is an absolute necessity.

Without an effective Sealift Readiness Program, DOD has greater justification for increasing the size of the MSC-controlled fleet, an option that would be opposed by the shipping industry. This possibility in itself is sufficient reason for the operators to work for an agreement that will gain the confidence of Pentagon planners. The role of the secretary of commerce in the call-up procedure must be strictly defined or eliminated because the possibility of his veto of a call-up, for any reason, introduces an unacceptable risk into contingency planning.[41]

The National Academy of Sciences study reports that operators believe the method of compensation is inequitable, and all evidence indicates they are correct. DOD should take the lead in reopening the question, but reworking the formula—that is, adding to the number of costs allowable for compensation—is probably only a short-run solution. Devising a standard list of allowable costs will be difficult, given different degrees of capital intensiveness among firms, and items that are allowable for compensation can be expected to change from time to time.

Less emphasis could be placed on arriving at a just compensation in predetermined monthly or quarterly payments. Instead, a standard formula—perhaps like the present formula—could be used for scheduled payments during a call-up, and a review board could determine any final payment needed to achieve equity among the parties. The board would consider such intangibles as loss of trade or good will and the cost of reestablishing routes and service. Equity law would be given equal standing with contract law in determining a fair compensation for the shipowner. Finally, it should be kept in mind that compensation is not paid until a vessel is taken, hence is

---

[41] In testimony before the Subcommittee of the Merchant Marine of the House Merchant Marine and Fisheries Committee in July, 1975, Mr. James J. Reynolds, president of the American Institute of Merchant Shipping (AIMS), stated the importance of certainty about call-ups under the Sealift Readiness Program. He called for a program setting forth "the conditions under which ships can be called, the procedures for establishing the charter rate, and perhaps the amount of time for which they must be committed."

not an item in MSC's annual budget. More important, however, is the recognition that when vessels are truly *needed*, MSC's balance sheet can be of only secondary importance.

Expectation of DOD cargo is the driving force behind the Sealift Readiness Program, but DOD cargo shipments have declined in the past few years from a high of approximately 28 million measurement tons to a projected 10 million. DOD cargo shipped by sea could decline until it is no longer advantageous for a firm to participate in the program. This possibility is not likely to happen immediately, but it is a real possibility. DOD and the Maritime Administration should explore alternative ways of acquiring privately owned shipping in nonmobilization contingencies. If new legislation is needed, it should be recommended to the Congress.

The National Defense Reserve Fleet

At the end of World War II, the United States government owned more than 5,000 merchant ships. To dispose of this gigantic fleet, Congress passed the Merchant Ships Sales Act of 1946, which authorized sale of this shipping, with preference being given to American citizens over foreign buyers. Authority to sell these vessels was to end on January 15, 1951, and ships not sold by that date were to become part of the National Defense Reserve Fleet (NDRF), as established under Section 11 of the act:

> Section 11 (a) The Commission shall place in a national defense reserve (1) such vessels owned by it as, after consultation with the Secretary of War and the Secretary of the Navy, it deems should be retained for the national defense, and (2) all vessels owned by it on December 31, 1947, for the sale of which a contract has not been made by that time. . . . A vessel placed in such reserve shall in no case be used for commercial operation, except that any such vessel may be used during any period in which vessels may be requisitioned under section 902 of the Merchant Marine Act, of 1936, as amended.[42]

The National Defense Reserve Fleet (NDRF) was to be maintained at nine anchorages located at James River, Va.; Baltimore, Md.; Hudson River, N.Y.; Wilmington, N.C.; Beaumont, Tex.; Mobile, Ala.; Astoria, Ore.; Olympia, Wash.; and Suisun Bay, Calif. On July 1, 1946, there were 1,421 ships in the fleet. Vessels in the NDRF

---

[42] U.S. Congress, *Merchant Ship Sales Act of 1946*, Public Law No. 321, 79th Cong., 2d sess., 1946, p. 10.

were government-owned, and responsibility for their preservation and maintenance was assigned to the Maritime Administration. But the Ship Sales Act of 1946 did not give unlimited discretion to the executive branch in using this shipping. Section 11 of the act limited the use of NDRF shipping to periods of national emergency, though, under special circumstances, private interests could charter NDRF vessels after a public hearing if necessary to maintain essential shipping services.

Operation of NDRF shipping in a national emergency was handled through a General Agency Agreement in which broken-out ships were assigned to the MSC in the Department of Defense. Responsibility for manning, provisioning, and repairing, and for general operation was assigned to the shipping firm holding the agreement. The government reimbursed the company for vessel expense plus a fixed fee.

Reserve ships made their first postwar contribution to the national security when 540 were broken out to support UN forces in the Korean War and to insure continued shipments of grain and coal to Europe and Asia. At the time of the Korean truce there were 1,932 vessels in the NDRF. Section 11 of the 1946 act did not mandate that all reserve ships be retained indefinitely, but only those deemed to have a national defense use. Ships in this category were placed on a retention list, which was reviewed periodically. The fleet has been thinned out as ships have been sold for scrap or for a nontransportation use when their preservation expenses could no longer be justified. NDRF ships were also used for surplus grain storage. Between 1953 and 1963, they stored more than 150 million bushels of wheat.

The closing of the Suez Canal in 1956 put a severe strain on much of the free world's shipping, not only on tankers sailing from the Persian Gulf to Europe and North America, but also on dry cargo ships. Shipping in all categories had earlier been in short supply and shipping rates had already been moving upward. When the canal closed, charter rates for tankers more than tripled while dry cargo rates increased by 40 percent. As a consequence, some 200 dry cargo vessels and thirty tankers were broken out of the NDRF.

The NDRF Role in the Vietnam War. The FY 1965 *Annual Report of the Maritime Administration* indicated there were 1,594 ships in the reserve fleet, a decrease of 474 from ten years earlier. On a priority list, 960 ships were under preservation.[43] The report for the following

---

[43] U.S. Department of Commerce, *Annual Report of the Maritime Administration 1965*, p. 33.

year reflected the Vietnam buildup—101 ships had been withdrawn from the NDRF at the request of the Military Sealift Command, most of them Victory-type ships. As in earlier emergencies, the operation of this shipping was under general agency agreement contracts with private operators. At the end of FY 1966, thirty-three firms were operating ships for the Southeast Asia sealift. Ultimately 172 ships would be withdrawn. They carried approximately 30 percent of government cargo to Vietnam between 1965 and 1969. All told, sealift moved 96 percent of DOD shipments during the Vietnam War. By and large, the aging reserve ships performed well, though there was some criticism of them.[44] Much of the criticism concerned the delays of cargo scheduled for American forces in Vietnam, but most delays were caused by a shortage of Vietnamese docking facilities or by crew shortages rather than ship breakdown. In November 1970, the last Vietnam reserve ship was returned to the NDRF.

The Post-Vietnam NDRF. On June 30, 1970, there were 1,027 ships in the reserve fleet. Four years later, there were only 487, including 134 Navy Department vessels.[45] There were 328, including Maritime Administration and navy ships, in the fleet preservation program, and scrap sales in 1975 further depleted that number. Of the ships for which the Maritime Administration had chief responsibility, the most important were 130 Victory-type and eight Seatrain-type vessels. These ships, all built during World War II and averaging more than thirty years in age, represent the last NDRF vessels with a national defense potential. And even this potential has been questioned by a number of DOD and industry officials.[46]

Most of these 138 ships were under dehumidification preservation and had cathodic hull protection.[47] In 1972, the Maritime Administration partially reactivated the S.S. *Greeley Victory* to determine the

---

[44] Lester Velie, "Our Leaky Pipeline to Vietnam," *Reader's Digest*, vol. 89 (December 1966), pp. 113–118.

[45] Department of Commerce, *Annual Report of the Maritime Administration 1974*, p. 41. These ships were at four fleet sites: James River, Va.; Beaumont, Tex.; Suisun Bay, Calif.; and Mobile, Ala. The Mobile site was closed in 1975.

[46] James J. Reynolds, president of the American Institute of Merchant Shipping, in testimony before the House Subcommittee on the Merchant Marine, could see no further use for these "essentially World War II vintage ships." Nor could Mr. Herbert Brand, president of the Transportation Institute, Washington, D.C., in his testimony before the same subcommittee.

[47] In dehumidification preservation, the interior of the ship is tightly sealed and a low relative humidity is maintained in the sealed spaces, to prevent corrosion. The underwater hull is protected from corrosion by a cathodic system, in which an electric current is applied through the water to the metal hull. The electric current renders the hull inert and unable to combine with oxygen to form rust.

effectiveness of the preservation techniques and to identify any bottle-necks in breaking out these ships. The test was deemed successful, and indicated ways of reducing the time and cost of returning a Victory ship to service.[48] Present estimates are that about $850,000 and twenty-one days are required to bring a mothballed vessel from the reserve fleet site to a loading berth. The Department of Defense, however, rejects this estimate, calculating instead that these vessels might require up to several months for reactivation and manning.[49]

In an effort to modernize the NDRF, Congress passed Public Law 93-605, the so-called Mariner Bill, which was signed into law on January 2, 1975. The bill provided two-year authority for the secretary of commerce "to acquire mariner class vessels . . . in exchange for obsolete vessels in the NDRF that are scheduled for scrapping." Under this bill, a firm that wanted to scrap a Mariner class vessel (thirty-five of which were built during the early 1950s) would turn it in to the NDRF and receive equivalent scrap tonnage. The Mariner is a 20-knot dry-cargo vessel, considered excellent for defense purposes. In the first six months of the program, however, no Mariners had been acquired, mainly because the shipping industry found the ships were still good revenue earners.

NDRF Summary. The type of ship now held by the Maritime Admin-istration in the NDRF—that is, the dry-cargo vessel capable of discharging its own cargo and accepting outsize military cargo, such as the army's main battle tank—is crucial to DOD contingency planning. Such ships—including the Mariner—are commonly called break-bulk vessels. Recently constructed American-flag shipping has been of the intermodal type, mainly the non-self-sustaining contain-ership. These highly specialized ships generally lack one or more of the defense-desirable features that the break-bulk vessels offer. As the American-flag, break-bulk ships become older and are replaced by intermodal ships, DOD sealift planning problems multiply. Retaining a break-bulk capability under the American flag ranks high among DOD priorities.

No less important to DOD planning is a viable NDRF, since the NDRF will ultimately be the home of break-bulk shipping. The requirement for an NDRF is not in dispute. DOD officials support the concept.[50] But the present NDRF probably does not meet DOD con-

---

[48] Department of Commerce, *Annual Report of the Maritime Administration 1972*, p. 16.

[49] Testimony of Dr. John J. Bennett before the Merchant Marine Subcommittee of the House Committee on Merchant Marine and Fisheries, June 5, 1975.

[50] Testimony of Dr. John J. Bennett, June 5, 1975.

tingency requirements which call for NDRF ships to be at a loading berth in a matter of days rather than months. An example would be the 1973 Middle East War.

Another problem is aging, even with the most modern preservation techniques. The retention-list Victory ships in the NDRF are more than thirty years old but have been operated for only about ten years. No one knows whether the ships can be kept another ten years or another fifteen. Research in this area would be advisable. Assuming the Victories and Seatrains will someday be replaced by newer ships, the question becomes how to fund the undertaking. Passage of the Mariner Bill was a first step, though there is some doubt that many ships will be acquired before the act's two-year limitation expires. In 1972, the Department of Commerce requested $33 million to purchase ten of the newer break-bulk ships for lay up in the NDRF. The proposal had considerable congressional support, but the Office of Management and Budget (OMB) ruled that such an acquisition was a military expense and should be part of the DOD budget. DOD did not request the funds.

OMB evidently does not object—and probably could not, given the explicit language of the Ships Sales Act of 1946—to the Maritime Administration having responsibility for preserving and maintaining ships already in the NDRF. This bureaucratic inconsistency would be of little note if the issue were not so important. Congress should decide whether the purpose of the NDRF is *military only*. And if it so determines, it should also decide whether maintenance of the NDRF should be in the navy budget. The shipping industry would probably oppose any transfer of the NDRF to DOD, however, fearing that at some future time NDRF vessels might be used to move defense cargo and to discipline rates if DOD thought them excessive. The well-documented congressional preference for privately owned shipping, however, could be expected to prevail. Another question is whether the Maritime Administration (or navy) should be given authority and funds to upgrade the NDRF by the outright purchase of vessels. Assuming the issue were resolved in favor of the Maritime Administration, then several collateral questions arise: Should the purchase of foreign ships be allowed? And should the Maritime Administration be given flexibility in using funds appropriated for vessel purchase to take advantage of "buys of opportunity" as they occur? Both questions would seem to require affirmative answers. The framers of the Merchant Marine Act of 1936 did not envision an NDRF, but it is now a fact and certainly a relevant one when considering the merchant marine as a naval auxiliary. Such consideration is long overdue.

Conclusion

This chapter has examined the concept of the merchant marine as a naval auxiliary and has made a number of points in support of the following recommendations.

(1) Merchant marine education should be reviewed thoroughly, either by the Congress or by a respected professional group, perhaps the National Academy of Sciences. Federal support for the U.S. Merchant Marine Academy and the six state academies should be examined, particularly in view of the anticipated oversupply of college graduates in general and the normal peacetime oversupply of merchant marine officers. The Maritime Administration should consider setting up courses to train merchant seamen and officers in underway replenishment techniques. Such courses will depend ultimately upon demand, but a beginning could be made. The navy and the merchant marine officers' unions must actively support the merchant marine naval reserve program, which is in the self-interest of both. Congressional encouragement in this respect would not be remiss.

(2) The national defense features provision of the Merchant Marine Act of 1936 probably should be used more extensively. The billions spent by the government in support of a merchant marine for national security justifies equipping merchant ships optimally to serve as military auxiliaries. At present, the Maritime Administration and the navy exercise joint control over the national defense feature program, but they sometimes disagree. Joint control presents no insurmountable difficulty provided that sufficient national defense feature funds are appropriated and that both agencies wholeheartedly support the program. The navy and the Maritime Administration probably should explore ways to insure that no otherwise suitable vessel leaves the shipyard without some specified minimum number of national defense features. Different vessels, of course, will have different national defense feature minimum specifications. Section 603 (b) of the Merchant Marine Act of 1936 might have to be expanded to include nonoperationally subsidized shipping.

(3) The entire underway replenishment role for merchant ships deserves more attention than it is getting. Much could probably be learned from the British (and the Soviet?) use of merchant navies in time of peace. Significant savings have been realized in shifting some navy underway replenishment responsibilities to the Military Sealift Command. Could even more savings be realized by shifting some of this new MSC responsibility to the privately operated union-manned merchant ships? The navy seems reluctant to do so, despite evidence

that such a role is possible—for example, the *Erna Elizabeth* demonstration. There is a growing realization within DOD that merchant ships, particularly containerships, will be required in a wartime underway replenishment role. The chief purpose of the Merchant Ship Naval Auxiliary Program is to determine precisely how such a role can be effected.[51] Denying an increased underway replenishment role to merchant ships in peacetime seems inconsistent with planning for their utilization in a war.

(4) The formula for compensating vessel owners for ships taken in a call-up under the Sealift Readiness Program should be revised. Because significant costs are not included in calculating compensation, shipowners are less likely to participate in the program. A longer-term equity approach, rather than one based strictly on a specified contract, merits consideration. Some thought should also be given to obtaining commercial sealift in a nonmobilization contingency, if too few ships are pledged under the Sealift Readiness Program.

(5) Congress should put the NDRF back on an even keel with a larger annual appropriation for purchase of additional ships. Although it plays a vital role in making the merchant marine a viable military and naval auxiliary, it has suffered a lack of funds. In the FY 1976 maritime authorization, the House Merchant Marine and Fisheries Committee recommended out of a total budget of $589,718,000 only $4,242,000 for the NDRF (less than the amount recommended for maritime training at the Merchant Marine Academy, Kings Point, which was $11,500,000, or for the state maritime schools, $5,808,000).[52] Maintaining a suitable merchant ship in the reserve fleet would cost the government no more than $10,000 annually in overhead and preservation expense. Breakout costs, even if they approached $1 million per ship, would still be a bargain when contrasted with the cost of a new or even a used ship.[53] And the breakout cost would not be incurred until an emergency occurred.

---

[51] In 1969 the chief of naval research asked the Maritime Transportation Board of the National Academy of Sciences to determine the feasibility of resupplying naval vessels at sea from commercial containerships. The results were published in National Research Council, *Containership Underway Replenishment: A Study of the Use of Containerships for the Underway Replenishment of Naval Vessels* (Washington, D.C.: National Academy of Sciences, 1971). Present navy effort in this respect is being conducted under the Merchant Ship Naval Auxiliary Program.

[52] U.S. Congress, House, *Maritime Authorization FY 1976*, Report No. 94-175, 94th Cong., 1st sess., p. 1.

[53] Estimated new construction costs in FY 1974 ranged from $24 million for a roll on/roll off type vessel to $205 million for a liquid natural gas (LNG) carrier. The estimated price for a break-bulk freighter built in the mid-1960s would be between $5 million and $6 million.

4

THE MILITARY
SEALIFT COMMAND

The Military Sealift Command, formerly the Military Sea Transportation Service, was established in 1949 to further armed forces unification, taking over the sealift mission of the Naval Transport Service and the Army Transport Service. Today MSC is an operating agency within DOD whose fleet commander is the executive agent of the secretary of the navy, who in turn is the single manager for all DOD sealift. MSC's primary mission is to support army, navy, marine corps, and air force sealift requirements in the event of war or a nonmobilization contingency. MSC also must plan for the expansion of peacetime shipping capabilities in time of emergency. Secondary missions include the worldwide direction of DOD cargoes by sea in peacetime and the operation of DOD vessels used primarily for nontransportation purposes, such as research ships (including oceanographic survey vessels and vessels in support of the NASA space program). More recently, MSC has taken over from the navy increasing responsibility for manning and operating the underway replenishment ships described in the previous chapter.

MSC operations are industrially funded: the command bills the services, including the navy, for the sealift services they use. The billings include all costs of providing the service with the exception of military salaries. The operation is supposed to break even, but in recent years deficits have been the rule rather than the exception. The proposed FY 1976 MSC budget was $985.5 million.[1] The size of MSC's operations has varied directly with the engagement of American forces overseas, as in Korea and Vietnam. After the Korean War, on January 1, 1954, the MSC-owned fleet numbered 255 vessels, or

---

[1] *The Budget of the United States Fiscal Year 1976* (Washington, D.C.: U.S. Government Printing Office, 1975), p. 334.

about 20 percent of the total active U.S. merchant marine. In addition, MSC had approximately 90 privately owned ships under charter, plus the use of 46 government-owned Maritime Administration ships, operating under general agency agreements.[2]

During the ten-year period between the military actions in Korea and Vietnam, the MSC-directed fleet declined in numbers as chartered shipping was returned to normal trades and NDRF vessels were laid up. MSC-owned shipping also decreased as older vessels were laid up or scrapped and not replaced. At the height of the Vietnam conflict, MSC-controlled shipping totaled 436 ships, including government-owned and commercially chartered vessels. As the American commitment in Vietnam ended, the size of the fleet declined. By 1970, it was down to 259 ships, and by 1972, it was smaller than at any time during the previous three decades. Moreover, the MSC-owned portion of this fleet was composed of aging ships, which would eventually require replacement unless the entire fleet were to become commercially chartered. DOD peacetime sealift requirements would then have to be met completely by chartered shipping and scheduled berth line service. In an emergency, this shipping would be augmented by vessels from the NDRF and ships committed under the Sealift Readiness Program. The Department of Defense, however, had reservations about the break-out time required for NDRF vessels and about the economic effect on a firm if its vessels were called up under the Sealift Readiness Program. Prompted by the aging MSC-owned ships and the uncertainty of shipping in a nonmobilization contingency, MSC in the late 1960s moved to replace some of its older tonnage.

Industry Issues

The private shipping industry, as might be expected, has been vitally concerned about MSC policies and the size of the MSC-controlled fleet.[3]

The Size of the MSC-Controlled Fleet. After unsuccessfully seeking procurement funds to replace T-2 tankers built in World War II, the navy in 1971 undertook to acquire some of this tonnage through a build-and-charter program. The navy solicited proposals from private industry to construct these tankers, which would be chartered by MSC for a twenty-year period with an option to renew. In essence,

---

[2] Wytze Gorter, *United States Shipping Policy* (New York: Harper and Brothers, 1956), p. 173.

[3] The composition of the controlled fleet and the means by which it expands in an emergency are discussed in the appendix.

MSC acquired equitable ownership of the vessel, though not the actual title. Because no government funds were involved in the construction of the vessel, navy procurement funds could go to the higher priority combatant ships. This program was implemented in June 1972, when agreement was reached for the construction and eventual chartering of nine 25,000 deadweight-ton tankers, at a total construction cost of $146,535,000.[4] All ships were scheduled to be in operation by 1976.

The attempt to replace MSC-owned dry-cargo tonnage met with less success. A proposal in the FY 1970 DOD budget to acquire thirty new cargo ships through a build-and-charter program (with a five-year charter, plus options for three five-year extensions) met with solid industry resistance. A typical objection was that the program would significantly increase the capacity of the MSC equitably owned fleet. The industry claimed that DOD peacetime shipping needs could be met by the berth lines, which were quite willing to make their ships available in a nonmobilization contingency. Quoting from an industry analysis:

> Of the present MSTS fleet, seventeen Victory ships will be removed from service by 1973. These represent a total annual vessel capability of 1.3 million measurement tons (MT). The thirty replacement ships have an annual vessel capability of 6.1 million MT, equivalent to eighty-one Victories. The net addition to the MSTS nucleus fleet is therefore nearly 5 million MT, the equivalent of about sixty-six Victories. To replace the capacity of the seventeen Victories, only six of the proposed new vessels would be required.[5]

Congress supported the industry position, and the proposal was dropped. A second attempt to acquire new MSC dry-cargo tonnage was made in 1973 when bids were sought for the construction of two multimission ships, one Lighter Aboard Ship (LASH) and one sea-barge (SEABEE) type vessel. This proposal had the endorsement of the DOD-sponsored interagency study, *Sealift Procurement and National Security*. DOD authorized procurement through the build-and-charter program in the fall of 1972, but orders for new merchant ship construction were then at a record high, and many American yards

---

[4] Comptroller General of the United States, *Build and Charter Program for Nine Tanker Ships* (Washington, D.C.: U.S. General Accounting Office, 1973), p. 12. This report also reviewed the build-and-charter method for procurement of other ships and made specific recommendations to Congress for its use by the Department of Defense.

[5] *Expansion of the MSTS Nucleus Fleet: Its Impact on the U.S. Merchant Marine* (New York: Harbridge House, Inc., 1969), p. 4.

were booked for two or three years. No acceptable bids were received.[6] The FY 1975 annual report of the Department of Defense renewed MSC's request for two multimission ships, one to be delivered in FY 1976 and the second in FY 1977.[7] In addition to LASH and SEABEE vessels, MSC was also considering roll on/roll off (RO/RO) ships. No bids were solicited in FY 1975, however, and the FY 1976 DOD annual report did not renew the request. Expecting close congressional scrutiny of its proposed $104 billion budget, DOD pared all but the most essential hardware requests.

In spring 1975, the MSC-controlled fleet was composed of sixty-five MSC-owned or long-term chartered vessels and fifty commercial ships under shorter-term charters. Of the MSC-owned ships, ten were cargo vessels, twenty-four were tankers, four were tugs, and twenty-seven were special-purpose ships. Of the commercially chartered ships, twenty-nine were cargo vessels, and the remainder tankers or special-purpose ships.[8] In summary, the MSC-controlled fleet in 1975 stood at 115 vessels, down considerably from its high of 436 ships during the war in Vietnam.

MSC's shipping operations could be eliminated entirely in the opinion of some maritime spokesmen. Former Maritime Administrator Andrew Gibson testified in 1971 before the Subcommittee on the Merchant Marine of the House Merchant Marine and Fisheries Committee:

> I have consistently advocated and continue to believe that the Government owned nucleus fleet should be composed only of special purpose vessels which are required to perform functions which the commercial fleet cannot perform. I further believe that military cargoes should be employed to support and strengthen berth line, common carriage shipping so that the commercial portion of this capacity can be diverted to military use in time of emergency.[9]

Later in 1971, before the Special Subcommittee on Transporta-

---

[6] A second factor was that the bid was for one-of-a-kind build, that is, to construct only one ship of each type. Gearing up to build a single ship is considerably more expensive and less profitable than building a series of ships.

[7] U.S. Department of Defense, *Annual Defense Department Report FY 1975*, p. 165.

[8] Rear Admiral Sam H. Moore, commander, Military Sealift Command, remarks before the New York chapter, National Defense Transportation Association, March 12, 1975 (unpublished).

[9] U.S. Congress, House, Subcommittee of the Committee on Merchant Marine and Fisheries, *Hearings, Cargo for American Ships, Part 1*, 92d Cong., 1st sess., 1971, p. 472.

tion of the House Committee on Armed Services, he responded to several questions by the committee's general counsel:

> Mr. Norris. What do you consider to be the role of the nucleus fleet?
> Mr. Gibson. I believe the cargo-carrying part of that nucleus fleet is totally unnecessary. I understand there are a number of ships, small icebreakers, research ships, and this is the bulk of the nucleus fleet that are engaged in noncommercial activities, and I think that is quite proper. . . . I think the Department of Defense can obtain tankers in any size, shape or number required from the commercial operator, providing they are willing to adequately compensate for them.[10]

Other authorities have defended the MSC-owned fleet. Writing in 1956, Wytze Gorter concluded:

> Without its own fleet, the MSTS would be entirely dependent upon private shipping. This would mean that the operating personnel aboard all ships carrying MSTS cargoes and passengers would be hired by private industry and be partly subject to the regulations of the relevant maritime unions. Under these conditions, a strike by unionized waterfront or shipboard employees could seriously cripple effective military operations. Military prudence demands a hedge against this risk.[11]

As Gorter points out, the bedrock argument for maintaining a DOD merchant marine is as a hedge against risk. Although the Department of Defense might insist on maintaining an MSC fleet of some size, it repeatedly stresses its almost total reliance on the merchant marine to meet its sealift requirements, both in peacetime and in time of emergency. Testifying before Congress in 1973, Rear Admiral John C. Chase, the commander of MSC, said:

> The British Navy has long utilized civilian manned logistics support ships in their Royal Fleet Auxiliary. Soviet merchant ships, operating in direct support of their fleet, are a common sight all around the globe. Such support is an example of

---

[10] U.S. Congress, House, Subcommittee of the Committee on Armed Services, *Hearings, Proposed Transfer of Military Sealift Command Functions to Military Traffic Management and Terminal Service*, 92d Cong., 1st sess., 1971, p. 6650.

[11] Gorter, *U.S. Shipping Policy*, p. 171. The issue of whether the merchant marine can be trusted as the nation's fourth arm of defense is far from settled, particularly with respect to the reliability of union crews. See the comment of Andrew Gibson, former Maritime administrator, in "Fourth Arm of Defense," *Seapower*, April 1976, p. 3.

new initiatives involving close substitutes which are designed to offset the adverse effects of Navy force reductions. Just about a year ago, Admiral Zumwalt wrote Chairman F. Edward Hébert with regard to Navy support for the merchant marine. In that letter he said: "Every naval task that can be performed by a ship of the merchant marine or the Military Sealift Command releases scarce Navy shipbuilding funds for combat ships and, where civilian manned ships can be used, military manpower requirements for support ships can be reduced to permit essential manning of combatant ships." This increased fleet support from MSC/merchant marine sources is in line with the concept of a high-low mix of forces about which Admiral Zumwalt has reported to you.[12]

The acting assistant secretary of defense (installations and logistics), John J. Bennett, stated in 1975:

First, I cannot overemphasize that the Department of Defense (DOD) supports and needs a viable U.S. flag merchant marine in peace and war. History books are full of references to the direct role played by U.S. flag merchant vessels in support of American forces overseas in time of war. In a major war, Defense would be almost entirely reliant on civilian shipping assets. In peacetime, the need is no less great, where the vast preponderance of our Defense cargo moves in U.S. flag vessels, much of it in berth line service, side by side with the freight of U.S. commerce. Indeed, a vital segment of the Defense Material Distribution System is in the hands of the U.S. flag maritime industry in peace and war.[13]

Procurement of Commercial Sealift. Another question of vital concern to the shipping industry is how MSC procures commercial shipping services in peacetime and in a nonmobilization contingency. There are several points of friction between MSC on the one hand and the shipping industry, sometimes together with the Maritime Administration, on the other. A report issued by the Special Subcommittee on Transportation of the House Committee of Armed Services on November 18, 1971, concluded:

The Military Sealift Command's relations with maritime in-

---

[12] U.S. Congress, House, Subcommittee of the Committee on Armed Services, *Hearings, HR 6722*, 93d Cong., 2d sess., 1973, p. 4110.

[13] Testimony of Dr. John J. Bennett before the Merchant Marine Subcommittee of the House Committee on Merchant Marine and Fisheries, June 5, 1975 (mimeographed).

dustry have been adversely affected by the Department of Defense policy that sealift procurement had to be on a competitive bid basis while at the same time the Department of Defense approved airlift procurement on a negotiated basis.

Under competitive bidding procurement procedures the merchant marine received non-compensatory revenues (compensation below actual costs) for carrying military cargo.[14]

This report was issued prior to completion of the 1972 *SPANS* study, which recommended changes in MSC procurement of commercial berth line service in peacetime. In response to one of these recommendations, a low bidder can no longer carry 100 percent of the DOD cargo moved on a particular route during the contract period, but is now limited to 50 percent and in a few cases to 75 percent.

Although the industry generally agreed with this modification, the Maritime Administration and others still believed the basic problem remained. Because MSC awarded cargo only on the basis of adequate service and the lowest rate where service is equal, a firm often submitted a low bid even if it failed to cover costs fully. The Maritime Administration found in August 1973 that the MSC method of procurement encouraged firms to bid so low that they threatened their own solvency in the long run. The administration recommended that the cargo allotments be revised to include all carriers submitting bids within a specified range.

> The proposed approach is to establish a maximum cargo percentage figure for each carrier on a route based on the relationship of his bids to the other bids on the route. It would permit the carrier with the lowest bids to carry the largest amounts of cargo and limit carriers with higher bids to proportionately smaller lots of cargo.[15]

In making its proposal to DOD, the Maritime Administration relied upon a *SPANS* recommendation that stated in part:

> The need for further changes to the DOD procurement system will depend upon the effectiveness of modifications already made (RFP 700) and any modifications subsequently deemed necessary. If existing or previous changes have been inadequate, then the case will exist for further change to competitive procurement or adoption of a cost based system.[16]

---

[14] U.S. Congress, House, Subcommittee of the Committee on Armed Services, *Report, Proposed Transfer of MSC Functions to MTMTS*, 92d Cong., 1st sess., 1971, p. 6838.

[15] U.S. Department of Commerce, *Analysis of Requirement for a Cargo Allocation System*, p. 26.

[16] U.S. Department of Defense, *Sealift Procurement and National Defense*, Executive Summary, p. 9.

DOD's response was contained in the *Annual Defense Department Report FY 1975*. It stated:

> Last August the Maritime Administration (MARAD), supported by the Federal Maritime Commission (FMC) and most of the berth line operators, proposed a cargo allocation system whereby all carriers offering service on a route would be assured of some cargo, with the amount allocated to any one carrier being a function of the bid spread. Their contention is that the MAX-MIN procedure causes large fluctuations in cargo allocations as the positions of the carriers in the bid rank change from one bidding cycle to the next. MARAD and FMC believe that these fluctuations create a "feast or famine" situation which is particularly harmful to those carriers in poor financial condition, which could lead to erosion of the sealift mobilization base. While we fully appreciate the concern of the Maritime agencies and the industry, we do not believe the evidence thus far presented is sufficiently convincing to justify either the relaxation of competition or the acceptance of the additional costs that would necessarily be involved.[17]

Demand for U.S. shipping services increased significantly in 1974, particularly in the North Atlantic. With commercial bookings up, the industry was less dependent on DOD cargo revenues, and the bid procurement controversy subsided. The issue is not dead, though. In this respect, there is no disagreement among any of the concerned parties. Basic positions have not changed. Under constant pressure to save funds, DOD cites the Armed Services Procurement Act of 1947, the basic law affecting DOD procurement, as justification for its bid procedures, which compel DOD to procure shipping services as economically as possible. On the other hand, the Maritime Administration and the Federal Maritime Commission, as well as most of the berth line operators, take the view that a feast-or-famine situation is in the interest of neither the companies nor the nation.

A second issue in commercial sealift procurement is how DOD will use private shipping under conditions of expanded requirements short of full mobilization. The question turns on the size of the MSC-owned fleet and DOD's order of priority for acquiring privately owned shipping. In a memorandum signed on July 1, 1954, by the Departments of Defense and Commerce, the so-called Wilson-Weeks agreement, the following principles were agreed upon.

---

[17] Department of Defense, *Annual Defense Department Report FY 1975*, p. 167.

[T]he Department of Defense and the Department of Commerce agree it is essential that the Department of Defense have under its exclusive custody, jurisdiction, and control, at all times, a nucleus fleet of size and composition to meet current conditions and military requirements. . . .

All merchant shipping capability required by the Department of Defense, in addition to that provided by the MSTS nucleus fleet, will be obtained, consistent with military requirements and prudent management, in the following order of priority:

(1) Maximum utilization of available U.S. flag berth space.

(2) Time or voyage charter of suitable privately owned U.S. flag merchant ships to the extent these are voluntarily made available by the maritime industry. Such time or voyage charters will be kept to the minimum necessary to meet requirements which foresight indicates cannot be met by U.S. flag berth operators.

(3) Shipping provided by National Shipping Authority under General Agency Agreement or other arrangement, or

(4) In the event suitable U.S. flag shipping is not available under conditions stated above, the Military Sea Transportation Service may employ foreign flag shipping only to the extent necessary to meet urgent military requirements.[18]

The Wilson-Weeks agreement has often been cited by DOD, the Maritime Administration, and the industry to make various points. In 1969, industry objected to MSC's proposal to build and charter thirty dry-cargo ships, claiming the proposal violated the agreement because it would effectively *expand* the MSC-owned fleet. On the other hand, the explicit statement in the agreement of DOD's "right" to maintain an MSC-owned nucleus fleet has been cited in opposition to proposals to abolish the commercial ship component of the nucleus fleet and reduce it to nontransportation, special-purpose ships. It is not surprising that revision of the Wilson-Weeks agreement comes up periodically. Both the shipping industry and the Maritime Administration have sought to reopen discussions with DOD. The 1972 *SPANS* study, concluded, "It is also apparent that the basic issues that the Wilson-Weeks Agreement sought to resolve are still present today. The inevitable conclusion is that the Wilson-Weeks Agreement must be updated."[19]

---

[18] U.S. Congress, House, Subcommittee on Merchant Marine of Committee on Merchant Marine and Fisheries, *Hearings, Cargo for American Ships, Part 1*, 92d Cong., 1st sess., 1972, pp. 308–310.

[19] Department of Defense, *SPANS*, Part 1, p. 29.

Some other questions were raised in the *SPANS* study:[20]

(1) At what rate will the MSC-controlled fleet be reduced after an expansion. DOD cites the preamble to the Wilson-Weeks agreement, which contains the phrase "consistent with military requirements and prudent management," when questioned about how fast the controlled fleet should be reduced. The issue was raised in 1970 when the industry claimed DOD was too slow in returning government-owned vessels to the National Defense Reserve Fleet.

(2) Since many MSC-owned vessels were built in World War II, and are now old, should DOD rely on a larger commercially chartered fleet and a smaller MSC-owned nucleus fleet?

(3) On the other hand, should berth liners—rather than a controlled fleet of chartered vessels—carry most DOD cargoes because they can operate more efficiently?[21]

Current Problems

MSC faces a number of problems, all of them important to its mission as manager of DOD sealift. Four of them are listed below, not necessarily in order of priority.

The continuing disappearance of break-bulk shipping from the U.S. merchant marine inventory. This is the type of shipping most adaptable to DOD requirements.

Severely constrained DOD budgets. In the present economic environment, navy ship procurement funds can be expected to be spent for combat ships or for ships of the Mobile Logistics Support Force, rather than for replacement of the MSC-owned fleet.

Continuing strained relations with the shipping industry and less rapport with the Maritime Administration. A number of points at issue have already been cited. Because DOD cargo movement has decreased to about 10 million measurement tons annually and the demand for ocean shipping remains cyclical, an adversary relationship between MSC and the industry will probably continue.

The rising cost of procuring commercial sealift services, either from berth line operators or through charters of commercial vessels.

---

[20] Department of Defense/industry issues are treated extensively in *SPANS*, Part 1, Chapter IV, "Current Issues," p. 24.

[21] Arguments supporting this position include: (1) commercial shipping carries cargo on both legs of a journey while military shipping is primarily outbound; (2) berth line operators utilize highly sophisticated cargo handling systems not available in military transportation systems; (3) DOD cargo offerings in many ports are less than a full shipload, thereby requiring a controlled ship to make many ports of call. See *SPANS*, Part 1, Chapter IV, "Current Issues," p. 24.

In a period of rising vessel-operating costs and fluctuating charter rates, MSC faces the doubly difficult task of pricing its services to users under a break-even concept while striving to avoid a deficit in its industrial fund.

Break-Bulk Shipping. The demise of the break-bulk ship in ocean transportation has become of increasing concern to DOD officials.[22] John J. Bennett, acting assistant secretary of defense (installations and logistics), said: "Of much concern, however, is the trend away from the versatile and flexible conventional general cargo vessel, carrying its own cargo handling gear and usable under essentially any circumstances and for almost the entire range of cargo characteristics."[23] The *SPANS* study stated: "New breakbulk freighters are not being constructed for U.S. registry, and beyond the early 1980's, breakbulk shipping appears unlikely to be available in significant quantity for military requirements unless it is especially built for, and at the expense of, the Defense Department."[24]

Part of the present break-bulk fleet is composed of ships built in the early 1960s. The problem is retaining these newer ships in the active U.S.-flag inventory when, in the words of *SPANS*, "Many of them already have become uneconomical in the trades for which they were built and are being replaced by container ships." The study went on: "The prospect is that more will be replaced by containerships in the near future and as additional barge carriers come into service, they will make inroads on the trades in which the modern freighters are now still able to make a profit."[25]

In mid-1975 there were 306 general cargo vessels in the privately owned U.S.-flag fleet. Of these, 158 were break-bulk ships, and only thirty-four were less than ten years old.[26] MSC had twenty-one general cargo ships under charter, fourteen of them the more modern break-bulk ships built in the 1960s. With a declining DOD sealift requirement, and a declining need for chartered ships, MSC's problem was how to preserve these break-bulk ships for use in a contingency. It would have been economical to return them to their owners at the

[22] Vice Admiral W. D. Gaddis, Deputy Chief of Naval Operations (Logistics), notes the problem of break-bulk ships in "Transportation Support for the Navy," *Translog: The Journal of Military Transportation Management* (October 1974), p. 4.

[23] Bennett, testimony before House Subcommittee on Merchant Marine, June 5, 1975.

[24] Department of Defense, *SPANS*, Part 3, p. I–18.

[25] Department of Defense, *SPANS*, Part 3, p. I–19.

[26] U.S. Department of Defense, Military Sealift Command, *Ship Register: July 1975*, p. 6.

expiration of the charter, but, with fewer trades in which the ships could be profitably employed, the owners might have disposed of them or converted them from break-bulk to an intermodal or even a tanker configuration.

One possibility was for MSC to establish a ready reserve fleet composed of the newer break-bulk freighters. Secretary of Defense Schlesinger suggested this in the *Annual Defense Department Report FY 1976*.[27] It was recommended to DOD by the navy, and the army considered it essential to the maintenance of a capability to meet contingencies short of mobilization.[28]

Renewal of the MSC-Owned Fleet. MSC has argued strongly for using build-and-charter as a method of procuring ships without using navy ship-procurement funds. But there is no difference to industry, particularly to the berth line operators, between an MSC-owned and an MSC equitably owned vessel. Both would carry DOD cargo that would otherwise move in privately owned shipping. Industry strongly opposes renewal of the active MSC-owned fleet by any method. In testimony before the House Merchant Marine and Fisheries Subcommittee on the Merchant Marine, James J. Reynolds, president of the American Institute of Merchant Shipping, recommended that a Ready Reserve Fleet should be developed to replace the nucleus fleet:

> In my opinion, there should be a Ready Reserve Fleet developed and placed under the control of DOD. It should be composed of such ships as are necessary to meet specified contingency situations. Some of these ships could be obtained by purchase and/or charter from the current active fleet, others would have to be constructed, perhaps under a build and charter program. They could be utilized in fleet exercises, in providing services to the very limited number of destinations not served by commercial operators, and in other ways consistent with their defined mission. I am certain that our industry would support such a Ready Reserve Fleet and would be pleased to work with DOD on its implementation.[29]

Industry hostility, coupled with the shortage of navy procurement funds, would seem to forestall revitalization of the MSC-owned

---

[27] Department of Defense, *Annual Defense Department Report FY 1976*, p. III–131.

[28] Fred Kornet, Jr., "Strategic Mobility: The Army Perspective," *Defense Management Journal*, April 1975, p. 17.

[29] James J. Reynolds, Testimony on the National Security and Economic Benefits of the United States Merchant Marine, before the Subcommittee on the Merchant Marine of the House Committee on Merchant Marine and Fisheries, July 9, 1975 (mimeographed).

dry-cargo fleet for the time being. The move toward some kind of ready reserve contingency fleet is no more or less than a recognition of these two facts.

Strained Agency-Industry Relations. An incident in 1974 particularly rankled the Seafarer's International Union. MSC obtained a bareboat charter of four union-manned tankers and replaced their union crews with civil service crews. The incident turned upon MSC's willingness to renegotiate the charter agreement with the vessels' owners, who needed the renegotiation for the firm's survival.[30] The company suggested a renegotiated consecutive voyage charter or, failing that, a time charter, both alternatives on a break-even basis. But MSC insisted upon a bareboat charter and manning by civil service crews. From the point of view of MSC, this decision was undoubtedly logical, but from a public relations viewpoint, the decision can only be termed a mistake. Union resentment has been prolonged.[31]

Another DOD decision that did little to improve DOD and MSC relations with industry was made in March 1975. The navy terminated the billet of naval adviser to the assistant secretary of commerce for maritime affairs. This position had been established in 1970 to provide closer cooperation between the navy and the Maritime Administration, and it was filled by Rear Admiral George H. Miller, a long-time advocate of the greatest possible use of merchant marine capabilities. The termination was protested by industry and union representatives and was sharply questioned in Congress. In a letter to Secretary of Defense Schlesinger dated March 5, 1975, Paul Hall, president of the Seafarer's International Union, stated:

> We are deeply concerned that the closing of the liaison office and the retirement of Admiral Miller is, in effect, a death blow to the hopes of all concerned for a means of fostering greater cooperation and a better working relationship between the Navy and the U.S. merchant marine.

> Perhaps more to the point, this act would be a clear repudiation of the agreement of September 1970 between the Secretary of the Navy and the Secretary of Commerce to establish a liaison office for the purpose of maximizing the merchant marine's contribution to the national defense.

---

[30] The vessel's owner, Falcon Tankers, Inc., was plagued by problems in the engine rooms of the four ships. Correcting the problems severely strained the financial position of the company, a situation that led to a request for renegotiation of its charter agreement with MSC.

[31] MSC later considered returning the four Falcon tankers to charter operation, that is, by a private company, under contract to MSC, that would man them with union seamen.

The navy pleaded budget constraints, however, and proposed assigning the director of logistics plans division in the Office of the Chief of Naval Operations the additional duty of acting as naval adviser to the maritime administrator.

Increasing Sealift Costs. Since 1973, the Military Sealift Command has faced rapidly increasing costs, particularly for fuel, which increased from approximately $4 a barrel on July 1, 1973, to almost $15 a barrel on April 1, 1974. Fuel costs composed about 40 percent of operating costs, compared with 15 percent two years earlier. Shipyard costs rose approximately 35 percent in 1974 and were still increasing afterward. Fuel and repair cost rises were the primary reasons cited by MSC for its approximately $77 million loss in FY 1974.[32]

With rapidly increasing costs and, in the case of fuel, where politics determines price as much as economic factors, MSC found it difficult to adjust its tariffs to break even. World economic conditions allowed, at best, the hope that industrial fund profits and losses would even out over a period of years. When a loss occurred in one year, however, the tariffs charged for user services had to be raised so that an offsetting profit would be realized the following year. This is current DOD practice, which also applies to the Military Airlift Command and the Military Traffic Management Command. User services, however, could never be sure how to allocate their transportation dollars efficiently, particularly between shipping by air or by sea. In a given year, MSC tariffs might be artificially high to make up a previous year's loss, while MAC tariffs might be artificially low because of an earlier year's profit. Thus, MSC's problem of coping with rising ocean transportation costs in a volatile economic environment cannot be considered independently of similar problems faced by MAC and MTMC.

Conclusion

The chief problem areas requiring DOD and MSC attention are how to maintain a contingency sealift capability, particularly a nucleus of break-bulk vessels, in a shipping world becoming increasingly intermodal, and how to restore relations among DOD, MSC, industry, and the Maritime Administration to the high point they reached under Admiral Elmo Zumwalt, as chief of naval operations, and Andrew Gibson, as maritime administrator.

---

[32] Comptroller General of the United States, *Letter Report B-181714* (Washington, D.C.: U.S. General Accounting Office, 1974), p. 1.

With respect to the first problem, MSC is considering creation of a ready reserve fleet of newer break-bulk vessels, and DOD and the Maritime Administration are considering plans to upgrade some thirty vessels in the NDRF to be time responsive to DOD needs in a contingency. If both plans are adopted, the United States will have in effect two NDRFs. Industry spokesmen support the MSC ready reserve fleet concept but expect these ships never to leave their berths carrying cargo except in a contingency. Supposedly, the ships would participate in fleet maneuvers and occasionally carry cargo to ports lacking commercial service. The likelihood of such a fleet coming into being, and being used in peacetime, however, cannot be ruled out. The Wilson-Weeks agreement would seem to mandate such use.

The second problem is solvable with a reasonable effort. The Maritime Administration is staffed by some of the most capable people in its history, and the same can be said of the Military Sealift Command. On the industry side, American shipping is making a comeback—slowly, but showing definite progress—and managers of most American shipping firms are demonstrably competent. The industry has adjusted to less—and, in many cases, no—operating subsidy in recent times. The above, however, has not always been the case. In the past, the Maritime Administration has been headed by purely political appointees who had little or no knowledge of shipping (and who seemed not to care), while MSC has had more than a few senior officers with little or no appreciation of the merchant marine. And, in years past, many American steamship firms accepted operating subsidies as a way of life, giving little thought to technological innovation and even less to the possibility of decreasing their dependence on the federal government.

The necessary elements, including a responsible maritime union leadership, are now present for a new era of improved relations between DOD, MSC, and industry.[33] The time may also be ripe for an entirely new structure within DOD for handling sealift and other transportation problems. Creating a completely new transportation environment will be discussed in the concluding chapters of this study.

---

[33] Lester Velie, "They're Finding Better Ways Than Strikes," *Reader's Digest* (March 1974), p. 42.

5
THE MILITARY AIRLIFT COMMAND

The present Military Airlift Command (MAC) is the successor to the Military Air Transport Service (MATS), which was organized on June 1, 1948, to provide a unified air transportation service for all DOD agencies. That service was created from the air force's Air Transport Command which decended from the army's Air Transport Command and the Naval Air Transport Service. The new organization was placed under the air force chief of staff. MATS was intended to be the primary supplier for DOD airlift requirements, but, six years after it was established, the Hoover Commission[1] found DOD operating three other passenger and cargo air lines, and assigning many aircraft to other commands. The navy was operating its Fleet Logistics Air Wings (FLOGWINGS) and a domestic air service (QUICKTRANS). The former was ostensibly a backup for MATS, and the latter, a domestic transcontinental airline providing service between naval activities on the East and West Coasts.

In addition to MATS, the air force was operating the Air Materiel Command (LOGAIR) to move priority materials worldwide. Out of a total DOD aircraft inventory of 4,028 transports in 1956, only 530 were engaged in MATS airlift activities.[2] The Hoover Commission recommended: "That the Secretary of Defense issue a superseding and controlling directive to eliminate the duplicating air transport services within the Department of Defense and merge the entire

---

[1] The Commission on Organization of the Executive Branch of Government (Hoover Commission) was established in accordance with Public Law 108, 83d Congress, and was approved July 10, 1953. The commission was made up of twelve individuals and chaired by former President Herbert Hoover.

[2] George M. Harmon, editor, *Transportation: The Nation's Lifelines* (Washington, D.C.: Industrial College of the Armed Forces, 1968), p. 141.

operation into Military Air Transport Service, except necessary administrative aircraft."[3]

On December 7, 1956, the secretary of the air force was designated single manager for all DOD airlift service, and MATS the operating agency. The service's airlift operations were to be industrially funded, that is, users would be billed for services provided. Additional transport aircraft were turned over to MATS, but neither the navy's QUICKTRANS nor the air force's LOGAIR was eliminated.[4] On January 1, 1966, MATS became the Military Airlift Command.[5] Changes in MAC's plane inventory and assigned personnel over the last two decades are indicated in Table 3.

The Airlift Service Industrial Fund has had the following fiscal year budgets: $716.9 million in 1974, $913.4 million in 1975, and $1,022.6 million (requested) in 1976.[6] This fund finances most airlift expenses, but not military pay or aircraft depreciation. In FY 1974, these two items amounted to $278 million and $270 million respectively.[7]

Contacts between the Military Airlift Command and Industry

The Military Airlift Command provides special-mission airlift for the President and aero-medical evacuation services for military personnel. It also operates the Air Weather Service and the Aerospace Rescue and Recovery Service. MAC's primary mission, however, is to provide the airlift for wartime deployment of American forces.

Since its beginnings as the army air force's Air Transport Service, MAC has participated in every war and contingency situation in which airlift was required. These operations included the 1948 Berlin airlift, the Korean War, the Vietnam War, and the resupply of Israeli forces following the Arab-Israeli conflict of October 1973.

---

[3] Commission on Organization of the Executive Branch of Government, *Transportation: A Report to the Congress* (Washington, D.C.: U.S. Government Printing Office, 1955), p. 59.

[4] The Military Airlift Command, however, had the responsibility for negotiating contracts for the QUICKTRANS and LOGAIR services. These all-cargo, fixed-schedule services operated only within the continental United States. In FY 1974 LOGAIR and QUICKTRANS shipments totalled approximately 140,000 and 48,000 tons, respectively.

[5] For a general, nontechnical history of MATS, see Clayton Knight, *Lifeline in the Sky: The Story of the U.S. Military Air Transport Service* (New York: William Morrow & Company, 1957).

[6] *The Budget of the United States Government 1976*, p. 336.

[7] Comptroller General of the U.S., *Airlift Operations of the Military Airlift Command*, p. 2.

Table 3

PLANES AND PERSONNEL OF THE MILITARY AIRLIFT COMMAND, 1954–74

	FY 1954	FY 1966	FY 1974[a]
Number of planes assigned	563	526	353
Type	C-54, C-121 C-135	C-135, C-141	C-141, C-5
Total personnel	103,268	100,000 (est.)	68,856
Assigned to strategic airlift functions	——	31,736	27,073

[a] In December 1974, C-130 tactical airlift forces of the Tactical Air Command were transferred to MAC. In a mobilization, MAC would also assume responsibility for tactical airlift forces assigned to the Air National Guard and the Air Force Reserves.

Sources: *Transportation: A Report to the Congress; Transportation: The Nation's Lifelines;* and *Airlift Operations of the Military Airlift Command During the 1973 Middle East War.*

MAC, like the Military Sealift Command, maintains an inventory insufficient for a sustained DOD airlift requirement and therefore depends upon augmentation by industry. Prior to the Korean War, this augmentation was obtained in the marketplace, that is, MAC chartered civil aircraft as the need arose. As demands of the Korean War intensified, however, a more formal arrangement became necessary.

The Civil Reserve Air Fleet. The Civil Reserve Air Fleet (CRAF) was established by an agreement between the secretaries of commerce and defense on December 15, 1951. Under this agreement DOD specified by aircraft type the supplemental civil airlift it would need in a national emergency. The Office of Emergency Transportation then assigned (by Federal Aviation Administration registration number) aircraft to the CRAF. Only preselected aircraft were assigned to CRAF. Remaining planes were assigned to the Civil Aeronautics Board, which was responsible for maintaining essential domestic airline service. The 1951 agreement called for the CRAF fleet to be activated in a general mobilization or war.

The initial CRAF program has been described as an "all or nothing" arrangement. In a general mobilization the entire CRAF would be activated, but in peacetime or in a nonmobilization contingency, the CRAF agreement could not obtain supplementary airlift, particularly if civil air fleets were fully employed in commercial service. Under these circumstances, the only option open to DOD was to procure supplemental airlift in the marketplace by soliciting formal bids. This method had the predictable consequence of insuring sufficient airlift when DOD demand was low and commercial demand static or declining. In this situation, bids tended to be low or even below actual cost. In a period of large DOD requirements, however, and when commercial demand was high or increasing, bids tended to be high or nonexistent. In many cases, DOD requirements were not fully met.

This method of procurement continued into the early 1960s when new procedures were adopted in response to congressional hearings and several DOD studies.[8] Their aims were to insure civil airlift responsiveness to DOD requirements under less than mobilization conditions and to encourage civil airlines to invest in aircraft suitable for DOD contingency requirements—that is, to expand civil air cargo capability.

A second memorandum agreement was signed by the secretaries of commerce and defense in 1963 providing for the procurement of civil airlift in stages ranging from normal peacetime needs to full augmentation of the CRAF fleet. The peacetime cargo and passenger contract between DOD and the civil carriers was to be the implementing device: DOD would contract with participating airlines to carry military passengers and freight, and, in return, the civil carriers agreed to make planes available, in either of two stages, in a situation less than national emergency. In the first stage the secretary of defense would activate the civil planes committed, and in the second stage the President would activate them. In both stages, aircraft would be available to DOD within twenty-four hours. In the third, or national emergency stage, the entire CRAF fleet would be activated by the President, a situation approximating a call-up under the original 1951 agreement. Airlines have the option of committing any part of their fleet to stages one or two, but, in practice, most airlines commit approximately equal numbers between the two stages.

In awarding its peacetime air movement contracts to civil carriers, DOD uses the following criteria: (1) a carrier's planes must be CAB certified, (2) DOD must approve the contracting airline, (3) service must be performed at rates approved by the CAB, (4) a no-work-

---

[8] For example, U.S. Congress, House, Subcommittee of the Committee on Government Operations, *Hearings, Military Air Transportation (1961)*, 87th Cong., 1st sess., June 1961, and U.S. Congress, House, Subcommittee of the Committee on Government Operations, 88th Cong., 1st sess., April 1963.

stoppage agreement must be in effect between the airline and its personnel, (5) DOD will consider the airline's ratio of civil to DOD revenue, and at least 45 percent of a carrier's total revenue must come from non-DOD sources, (6) DOD will review the type and quantity of aircraft committed to the first stage, and (7) DOD will consider the carrier's cost of operations in relation to other carriers.[9]

Using the above criteria—basically the type and quantity of aircraft committed to the first stage and a carrier's relative operating costs—an award index is developed that determines the amount of DOD business awarded to a particular airline. American carriers committed 246 long-range international aircraft—156 cargo or passenger-cargo convertible and 90 passenger only—to the CRAF program in 1975.[10] An additional 100 shorter-range planes were also committed, both for international flights and for service to Alaska and Hawaii. Both DOD and the industry have generally endorsed the revised CRAF procedures. The first stage of the CRAF program has never been implemented because DOD has been able to supplement its airlift requirements satisfactorily under normal peacetime contract procedures.

Who Shall Carry DOD Peacetime Air Cargo?

The CRAF program provides both a means for DOD to obtain supplementary airlift in emergency situations and a financial inducement for carriers to invest in aircraft suitable for defense. But the CRAF program provides no guidance on allocating peacetime DOD cargo and passengers between MAC aircraft and the civil air carriers. The Hoover Commission Task Force on Transportation addressed the question in its 1954 report, recommending that commercial carriers be used whenever possible:

> To build a military air transport service capable of meeting all air transport needs in wartime would involve enormous sums. The capital costs of new transport aircraft are about the same for military or civil use. Military operating costs are reported as lower than private airline operating costs for the same type of aircraft. However, military operating costs do not include depreciation, crew salaries, interest on Government funds used to purchase the aircraft, taxes, and other

[9] Department of Defense, *SPANS*, Part 4, pp. C–4, 5.

[10] Department of Defense, *Annual Defense Department Report FY 1976*, p. III–123. Long-range international passenger and cargo planes include the Boeing 747F, 747, and 707-300C, and the McDonnell-Douglas DC-8-50F, DC-8-60F, DC-9, DC-10, and DC-10-30AF.

cost items of private operators. Moreover, the great economy of the civil air fleet and their trained personnel lies in productive peacetime use while serving as an immediately available reserve for emergencies. . . .

We do not have the resources to maintain within the Military Establishment in time of peace all the transport planes and personnel which would be needed in time of war. The commercial airlines with their bases, equipment, and personnel constitute an air transport reserve for war. They must be encouraged to expand.[11]

Recommendation 13 (c) of the report stated:

That the peacetime operations of the integrated Military Air Transport Service be restricted and realistically limited to persons and cargo carefully evaluated as to necessity for military air transportation and, only after commercial carriers have been utilized to the maximum practicable extent, should transportation on Service carriers be authorized.[12]

Designating the air secretary the single manager for all DOD airlift resulted in a significant, though not complete, consolidation of the military airlift resources under the Military Air Transport Service. DOD was less enthusiastic about the task force recommendation that more air cargo be assigned to commercial carriers. In the years following the Hoover Report, from 1956 to 1959, congressional committees continually reaffirmed that, whenever practical, commercial carriers should move DOD air cargo and passengers. In 1958, after a lengthy review of relations between DOD and the civil air industry, the Military Operations Subcommittee of the House Government Operations Committee made these recommendations:

The Military Air Transport Service should concentrate on outsize and special-cargo traffic and technical missions, leaving to the civil air carriers the primary responsibility for the transportation of passengers and more conventional kinds of cargo.

The applicable military directives and regulations should be redrafted to eliminate the preferential position of the Military Air Transport Service in peacetime military airlift and to establish, consistent with other recommendations in this report, a full partnership role for civil carriers in moving peacetime military traffic and in contributing to war readiness through the Civil Reserve Air Fleet.

---

[11] Commission on Organization of the Executive Branch of Government, *Transportation*, pp. 56–59.

[12] Ibid., p. 59.

Table 4

ALLOCATION OF MILITARY AIR CARGO, 1960–70

Fiscal Year	Total Tons of Cargo	Commercial	Percent
1960	168,787	17,581	10.4
1961	159,700	26,409	16.5
1962	181,707	73,669	40.5
1963	184,359	69,077	37.4
1964	196,841	43,683	22.1
1965	253,392	66,067	26.0
1966	338,368	102,106	30.1
1967	599,202	201,905	33.6
1968	679,079	163,073	24.0
1969	725,322	147,603	20.3
1970	658,643	103,991	15.7

Source: U.S. Congress, Senate, Committee on Commerce, *Report: Transportation of Government Traffic by Civil Air Carriers*, 92d Cong., 1st sess., November 19, 1971, p. 13.

In the event the applicable military directives and regulations are not redrafted to eliminate the preferential position of the Military Air Transport Service and an effective program is not developed for expanding the use of commercial services, the Congress should adopt appropriate legislation to achieve these objectives.[13]

During the 1960s, the cargo capacity of both the MATS and the CRAF fleet expanded significantly. MATS acquired a large fleet of C-141s, while civilian carriers invested in turbine-powered cargo and cargo convertible aircraft, such as the Boeing 707 and the McDonnell-Douglas DC-8. As might be expected, during economic downturns, a considerable part of this new and expensive civil airlift capability was idle. When this occurred, the question of who should carry DOD air cargo was raised again. Table 4 indicates how military cargo was allocated to MATS and the commercial carriers during the 1960s.

In May 1971, Senator Warren Magnuson (Democrat, Washington) introduced S. 1821 which stated:

Whenever the Department of Defense moves persons or property by air between a place in the United States and a

---

[13] U.S. Congress, House, Committee on Government Operations, *House Report No. 2011. Military Air Transportation*, 85th Cong., 2d sess., June 26, 1958, pp. 5–6.

place outside thereof or between two places both of which are outside the United States:

(1) To the fullest extent practicable, such persons and property (except persons and property that must move in military aircraft because of special military considerations which by their nature preclude the use of civil aircraft, or because of security, or in the case of property because of limiting physical characteristics such as size or dangerous properties) shall be transported by air carriers participating in the civil reserve air fleet program and holding certificates under section 401 of this Act to the extent allowed by such certificates or by regulation or exemption of the Civil Aeronautics Board and to the extent such carriers are available at rates established under this Act.

(2) As a minimum, at least 50 per centum of the annual gross tonnage (measured in ton-miles) of all property moved by the Department of Defense by air between such places shall be transported by air carriers participating in such program and holding such certificates to the extent such carriers are available at such rates.[14]

The House Committee on Commerce reported the bill favorably, though, after amendments, the 50-percent share for civil carriers was reduced to 40 percent. The report that accompanied S. 1821 was quite critical of DOD's use of the CRAF fleet:

What has happened is obvious. There has been a complete reversal of policy. After inducing the civil carriers to acquire substantial cargo capacity by offering them a fair share of military cargo business, the Department of Defense has simply pulled the rug out.

In a memorandum submitted by the Air Force to Chairman Cannon on April 7, this reversal of policy is quite clearly revealed. That memorandum states that "Efficiency and economy dictate the use of this (MAC) capability to satisfy logistic support requirements." (p. 1.) It further states that "the primary role now developing for the civil air carriers is to replace the MAC aircraft on their worldwide DOD logistic support routes when they are diverted to carry out a wartime deployment." (p. 2.) Otherwise, the only role contemplated for the civil carriers, so far as international cargo is concerned, is "to satisfy peak international cargo demands." (p. 3.)

In "The Role of MATS in Peace and War," the very first

---

[14] S. 1821, "A Bill to Amend the Federal Aviation Act, as amended, with respect to the transportation of Government traffic by civil air carriers of the United States," 92d Cong., 1st sess.

item listed under the heading "Presidentially Approved Courses of Action" reads as follows:

> 1. That MATS be equipped and operated in peacetime to meet approved military hardcore requirements in a general war and such other military requirements as cannot be met adequately by commercial carriers on an effective and timely basis. (p. 5.)

The Air Force has now turned this policy on its head. It proposed to use the *civil carriers* only for "such other military requirements as cannot be met adequately by *the military.*"[15]

Congress did not act on S. 1821, and in 1973 similar bills were introduced in the House and Senate (H.R. 5085 and S. 1350). Both bills set a mandatory amount of DOD cargo for air carriers participating in the CRAF program. The House bill proposed 50 percent to the civil carriers, and the Senate bill required 40 percent.

In FY 1973, MAC moved 1,411,211 passengers and 451,142 tons, with commercial carriers handling 1,220,862 passengers (81.2 percent) and 84,674 tons of cargo (13.5 percent).[16] Since 1973, total DOD air cargo movement has declined, particularly since the American withdrawal from Vietnam. With a smaller total, commercial air carriers are seeking a larger share of DOD air cargo, but no bill that would mandate a specific share of DOD air cargo to the commercial airlines has cleared Congress. The airlines' case was stated by Paul R. Ignatius, president of the Air Transport Association, in a special transportation issue of the *Defense Management Journal*. He said:

> A key source of economic strength for the airlines lies in moving increasing amounts of traffic, *including routine military traffic*. Therefore, it makes sense that the Department of Defense should make substantial use of the commercial airlines in moving routine traffic, and that the use of military transports be concentrated on the specialized military missions for which they have been designed.
>
> Military cargo traffic, however, has been declining for the commercial airlines. The decline is far sharper than could be attributed solely to the winding down of U.S. military activity in Southeast Asia. The decline has come in percentage

---

[15] U.S. Congress, Senate, Committee on Commerce, *Report: Transportation of Government Traffic by Civil Air Carriers*, 92d Cong., 1st sess., November 19, 1971, p. 13.

[16] U.S. Department of Defense, Military Airlift Command, *Airlift Service Management Report, July 72/June 73*, pp. 14–15.

of available military traffic going to commercial airlines, as well as in tonnage.[17]

Aerial Ports and Terminals

In 1975, MAC was operating seventeen major cargo and passenger aerial ports, six of them in the continental United States. Guam, Hawaii, and Alaska had one each, and the remaining eight were in foreign countries. Between 1973 and 1975, construction in the United States included new passenger facilities at Travis Air Force Base, Calif.; Hickham Air Force Base, Hawaii; and McGuire Air Force Base, N.J. Freight terminal facilities have recently been completed or upgraded at Charleston Air Force Base, S.C.; at Travis Air Force Base, and at Dover Air Force Base, Del.

In a national emergency, facilities at designated commercial airports would be available to service MAC flights, but to what extent might MAC share commercial airport facilities in peacetime?[18] The federal government is already committed to massive financial assistance to the nation's commercial airports. In FY 1975 this amount was estimated to be $316 million, with an additional $1.45 billion from state and local governments. These funds were to be spent on airports *only*. Under the Airport and Airway Development Act of 1970, the federal government in 1975 programmed outlays of $2.1 billion for the airway system and for airport grants.[19] Perhaps MAC cannot utilize or partially utilize commercial airports in peacetime, but, with the large federal expense involved in maintaining the nation's commercial airports, the burden of proof would seem to fall upon DOD. DOD sealift cargo moves through commercial terminals and containerports, and the trend is toward even more use of civilian facilities.

Some savings presently are possible in MAC operations at its own aerial ports. A 1975 General Accounting Office report concluded: "MAC aerial ports are currently staffed to provide wartime strategic airlift capability rather than to meet current peacetime workloads. As a result, MAC is spending about $17 million annually for the additional personnel."[20]

---

[17] Ignatius, "Let Airlines Play an Optimum Role," *Defense Management Journal*, p. 14.

[18] Adjoining or closely proximate military and commercial airports are not new. A number have existed for a long time, for instance, the Charleston Air Force Base adjacent to the commercial airport in Charleston, S.C.

[19] *Budget of the United States Government (Annex) FY 1975*, p. 680.

[20] Comptroller General of the United States, *Letter Report B-133025* (Washington, D.C.: U.S. General Accounting Office, 1975), p. 6.

Since the disengagement from Vietnam, the air force has been reevaluating its peacetime active-duty staffing requirements at MAC bases. It might also explore the feasibility of some MAC use of present and future commercial airports.

Joint civil and MAC use could be considered when new airport construction is planned, even if it is not feasible to combine present facilities. New airports are likely to handle much more freight, given the large projected increase in intercity and international air freight movement. Common use of newer air freight handling facilities and technology could result in savings.

Airlift in Contingencies

MAC, the Air Force Reserve, the Air National Guard, and CRAF provide sufficient airlift capability to meet DOD peacetime requirements. In most years, there is an excess capability. Deputy Secretary of Defense David Packard made this point in 1971:

> The size of our active military airlift is determined so that it, together with the full capacity of our Reserve and National Guard airlift forces, and the capacity of those suitable U.S. civil aircraft which the Department of Transportation will allocate to the Civil Reserve Air Fleet, can meet peak contingency airlift needs. *These contingency needs far exceeds the Department of Defense peacetime airlift needs* [italics supplied].[21]

When there is excess capability, the question quickly becomes, Whose planes shall be grounded? The air force maintains that MAC planes should form the core, or initial airlift capability, in a contingency and that this core must be maintained in peacetime. The aircraft utilization rate (number of hours the aircraft flies per time period) should be sufficient, the air force says, to provide the minimum crew training necessary for wartime readiness. Civilian operators quote DOD's own words that MAC capability is insufficient to meet a sustained emergency and that DOD must rely on the CRAF. The civilian operators argue that it is equally, if not more, important to maintain an economically viable civil air industry. Both points of view have merit. Civil air carriers were reluctant to commit aircraft voluntarily to the 1973 Israeli resupply effort unless the CRAF agreement was formally invoked. The agreement, however, was not invoked, so the carriers can hardly be faulted for making the decision they considered

---

[21] Senate, *Transportation of Government Traffic*, p. 29.

correct. Moreover, the companies did make planes available to carry routine DOD cargo to Europe and the Pacific, thereby freeing MAC planes for the Israeli airlift.

The most important considerations, however, are how quickly CRAF planes can be available and whether CRAF capabilities match DOD contingency needs. The CRAF agreement calls for planes to be made available within twenty-four hours. Presumably, in some instances, this time could be shortened, but nothing on record indicates that MAC considers early plane availability a serious problem.[22] As to plane capability, DOD has less concern about its ability to airlift troops than about a perceived shortfall in MAC and CRAF cargo lift capability. This concern was indicated when Secretary of Defense Schlesinger proposed a major expansion of strategic cargo airlift capacity in DOD's FY 1975 annual report.

The Airlift Enhancement Program

DOD's FY 1975 proposal to expand strategic airlift capacity was three-pronged. First, wartime utilization rates of the C-5A and C-141 were to be raised by increasing active force crew ratios, maintenance personnel, and war reserve replacement spares. Second, the C-141s were to be modified to increase their usable payloads. This would be done by lengthening the fuselage by 280 inches and adding an in-flight refueling capability. Third, and of most interest here, civil aircraft were to be modified to make them more compatible with DOD wartime requirements. The FY 1975 annual report stated:

> Moreover, we believe that a large amount of additional airlift capacity can be acquired at a far lesser cost through a Government-financed program for the modification of existing civilian wide-bodied passenger aircraft (Boeing 747s and McDonnell-Douglas DC-10s) to a convertible (cargo-passenger) configuration, and for the operation of these modified aircraft under the CRAF program.[23]

The program would have added 110 cargo-convertible 747s (or DC-10 equivalents) to the CRAF fleet. This supplement to MAC's C-141s and C-5As would go a long way toward meeting DOD requirements for a rapid deployment of U.S. forces. Several significant

---

[22] Early plane availability, however, must be matched by early cargo availability. It goes for naught if the carrier is ready and there is no cargo to load.

[23] Department of Defense, *Annual Department of Defense Report FY 1975*, p. 162. Proposed modifications included installation of a nose visor door or a large side loading door or both, strengthening the upper cargo deck, and installation of a cargo-floor weight-distribution system.

problems, however, were identified. The first problem was how to provide an incentive for airline participation. Again in the words of the FY 1975 annual report:

Heretofore, we have relied upon the award of peacetime airlift contracts as the principal inducement for the air carriers to participate in the CRAF program. With the sharp decline in contracted airlift following the withdrawal of U.S. forces from Vietnam, there will not be enough Defense business to provide the necessary incentives for an expanded CRAF program.[24]

A second problem was the cost of modification, estimated at $5.6–6.6 million for a 747, depending upon the extent of the modification. In addition, the airlines would require compensation for the time the plane was out of service while being modified. And finally, carriers would have to be compensated in some way for additional operating costs incurred because of the modification. It was estimated that "taking all of these factors into account, the cost to the Government could amount to about $9–10 million per modified 747."[25] Major General Paul F. Patch, director of transportation for the air force, noting DOD's large in-hand airlift capability, summed up the justification for the air enhancement program:

Despite this impressive capability, it is not sufficient to satisfy the Secretary of Defense's objective of being able to move large-scale reinforcements to Europe during the critical early weeks of a NATO-Warsaw Pact conflict. Specifically, he felt that the most impressive deterrent to a Warsaw Pact attack on NATO would be our ability "to put down in Europe a fully-equipped combat-ready division (including support forces) every few days." To this end he felt that a major expansion of our airlift capacity deserved a high priority in the allocation of resources.[26]

Congressional Consideration. DOD's FY 1975 proposal for an airlift enhancement program was only partially successful. Congress approved $25 million to begin the modification of a C-141 into a stretched prototype configuration, but funds were denied for increasing and modifying the long-range CRAF fleet. Congressional committees did not object to increased airlift capability, but they criticized DOD

---

[24] Department of Defense, *Annual Department of Defense Report FY 1975*, p. 163.

[25] Ibid., p. 164.

[26] Paul F. Patch, "Airlift Enhancement: Issues and Answers," *Translog: The Journal of the Military Traffic Management Command*, June 1974, p. 3.

for not doing its "homework," that is, for not coming up with a more detailed requirement and a better analysis of the contribution a modified 747 or DC-10 could make.

The airlift enhancement program was proposed again in DOD's FY 1976 annual report, for the most part with the same rationale. The cost to modify 100 DC-10 and 747 aircraft was estimated at $6.8 billion. Of this amount $22 million was requested in the FY 1976 budget.[27]

One new thought was gently put forward. In a roundabout way, DOD asked that Congress consider subsidizing long-range aircraft for the same reasons it provides subsidies for the merchant marine:

> The Defense Department has relied for some time on the U.S. maritime industry to provide the bulk of our sealift forces in a time of national emergency. The Congress, in recognition of this fact, has authorized subsidies for the shipping industry to ensure the availability of these assets in emergencies. We believe that similar reliance can be placed on the civil sector for airlift support in emergencies, now that large numbers of wide-bodied, long-range aircraft suitable for use in military unit deployments are available. Reliance on the civil sector for our emergency lift needs permits us to achieve savings in procurement and, even more significant over the long term, savings in operating and maintenance costs.[28]

Some Questions. The airlift enhancement program has attracted considerable congressional interest, and it will certainly receive more. Questions receiving attention include the following:

(1) Is rapid deployment of American forces to Europe the only contingency that would require a significant increase in DOD cargo airlift capability? If so, does such a capability imply a significant cut in American forces in Europe? In other words, is a capability for rapid redeployment of U.S. forces to Europe to be a substitute for an American presence at some future time? The Israeli resupply effort demonstrated the American airlift capability in a real contingency, but the CRAF fleet was not used. What intermediate contingencies may be foreseen between the Israeli type of airlift and a major deployment of forces to Europe? Would twenty-five or fifty or seventy-five modified civil long-range aircraft suffice?

(2) What consideration has been given to shifting a greater por-

---

[27] Department of Defense, *Annual Department of Defense Report FY 1976*, p. III–129.

[28] Ibid.

tion of a NATO redeployment effort to sealift, including some redeployment of troops? In the Vietnam War, 95 percent of the cargo moved to Southeast Asia was shipped by sea, and in the Israeli resupply effort the figure was 74 percent. DOD emphasizes that sustaining NATO forces in a European war would be primarily a sealift responsibility. Assuming some supplies for redeployed American forces are already pre-positioned in Europe, to what extent will modified civil aircraft be used to move troops rather than military cargo? The CRAF part of the airlift enhancement program seems intended to increase the cargo capability of the planes rather than the troop-carrying capability. What is the trade-off in cost between pre-positioning an acceptable level of equipment and supplies in Europe and cutting back or eliminating a $6.8 billion airlift modification program? This question, like the first, cannot be answered without congressional review of DOD's war plans—an event that is unlikely to occur. The questions are posed here only because they are relevant in considering the need for an expanded CRAF. Remaining questions will be more pertinent to the economics of maintaining and utilizing an expanded CRAF fleet in peacetime.

(3) In 1975, U.S. commercial airlines committed 246 long-range aircraft to the CRAF program. How many can be expected to be committed in 1980? In 1990? The answer would seem to depend upon how rapidly the demand for world air cargo service will grow over the next ten or fifteen years and to what extent U.S. carriers share in this growth. (A second consideration, whether DOD can persuade the carriers to continue to commit a significant number of their planes to CRAF, given declining DOD air cargo movement, will be discussed in the chapters on issues and problems and on managing defense transportation.) The market for world air cargo service is expected to expand rapidly over the next twenty years. The annual average growth rate for the U.S. international airlines share of world air cargo until 1987 is estimated at 13.5 percent. The International Civil Aviation Organization estimates that American international carriers will move from a projected 3.3 billion revenue ton miles in 1976 to a projected 14.3 billion in 1987. As the U.S. civil air cargo fleet grows and as air cargo increases, many modifications sought in the airlift enhancement program, such as strengthened decks and loading accommodations for outsize cargo, could be incorporated into the civil fleets as a result of marketplace economics. DOD's main problem then would be to entice this additional capacity into the CRAF program. The airlift enhancement program thus may rest more on near-term contingency requirements than on contingencies in ten or fifteen years.

(4) If DOD requires additional airlift capacity before civil aviation

introduces planes meeting DOD requirements in the way merchant ships do, then consideration should be given to building a version of national defense features into future plane construction, rather than modifying present planes. Incorporating national defense features into new merchant ship construction costs significantly less than later modification of the ship, and the same may be true of aircraft, though the modified plane might have additional operating costs. In any case, the possibility of realizing savings by incorporating national defense features during aircraft construction is worth examining.[29]

(5) In its FY 1976 annual report DOD seemed to propose a permanent operating subsidy for aircraft with national defense features. Who would pay this subsidy in the long run? DOD might be willing to pay initially to get the program started, but would it be willing to earmark a part of its budget continually for this purpose? Would the Department of Transportation or the Civil Aeronautics Board be willing to include such a subsidy in its annual request for appropriations?

(6) If a subsidy is eventually paid, could it constitute the difference between an airline staying in business and its liquidating? Put another way, What would be the likely result if two American-flag carriers, one subsidized and the other not, came upon hard times? Would not the subsidized firm be more likely to survive even though it might be the less efficient? The Merchant Marine Act of 1936 in effect divided the American merchant marine into subsidized and nonsubsidized sectors. By 1960, all lines were subsidized or had applied for subsidy. Operating differential subsidies for merchant ships may differ from a compensating subsidy for national defense feature equipped aircraft, but lessons can be learned from the merchant marine experience.[30] A companion concern is whether aircraft modified at government expense would have an unfair advantage over non-modified aircraft in carrying commercial outsize cargo. This question has been raised by the supplemental carriers. In response, the air force is considering requiring reimbursement of modification costs if modified aircraft are used to transport cargo. This might be equitable, depending upon how much of the modification cost is reimbursed, and over what period.

(7) A question that will be mentioned here and considered in a later chapter is, What is the effect of containerization on DOD cargo

---

[29] Manufacturers would probably be required to offer two versions of the plane. One would include national defense features, the other, presumably for non-U.S. airlines, would not.

[30] See Clinton H. Whitehurst, Jr., "The Merchant Marine Act of 1936: An Operational Subsidy in Retrospect," *Journal of Law and Economics*, vol. 8 (October 1965), p. 223.

movement? By 1976 DOD peacetime cargo moved in containers will approach an estimated 80 percent of the total. Many DOD items will never lend themselves to containerization—the M-60 main battle tank, for instance, and self-propelled guns—but many others probably can be containerized by using flat racks.[31] In terms of the airlift enhancement program two questions are relevant. First, would the DOD-proposed modifications make the planes more or less efficient in handling containerized cargo? And second, How much DOD cargo can ultimately be containerized?

Conclusion

The concept of a single supplier for airlift has come a long way since the Military Air Transport Service was organized in 1948. That it still has some way to go is illustrated by an internal skirmish at the Pentagon over continued navy operation of its own air transport service.

> In 1948, shortly after the department [DOD] was created as the unifying, central authority over the three services, the Military Air Transport Service, now known as the Military Airlift Command, was established as the Defense Department's airline for all the services. In principle, the airline, managed by the Air Force, was to be responsible for air movement of all cargo and personnel of the individual services, which paid the airline for the service.
>
> The Navy, which tends to be the most independent of the services, continued, however, to operate its own independent air service, insisting that it could not rely on the Military Airlift Command to meet the high priority needs of the fleet and Marine Corps. In the present fiscal year, the Navy is operating a fleet of 84 transport aircraft at a cost of $60 million.
>
> The issue, long an irritant to the Air Force, came to a crisis when the Navy wanted to purchase new jet planes, principally DC-9s to modernize its air transport fleet, much of which consists of DC-3s and DC-6s left over from the post-World War II period.[32]

The Defense Department questioned the navy request on the grounds that it duplicated MAC routes, and suggested instead that the navy give up its fourteen DC-9s and rely on MAC service. The

---

[31] A flat rack essentially is an open container consisting of platforms with corner posts and end frames that can support loaded racks stacked in cells above them.

[32] *New York Times*, June 13, 1975, p. 44.

proposal also would have eliminated the naval reservists who fly naval transports, so a reserve-sensitive Congress became involved. The result was, "The Navy will be permitted to keep 14 DC-9s and seven C-130 turbo-prop transports on the condition that their use does not compete with services offered by the Military Airlift Command."[33] Navy reservists were authorized to continue flying fifty of the older planes until 1977 to give MAC sufficient time "to develop plans to meet the Navy's air transport needs."

The Military Airlift Command faces many of the same problems as the Military Sealift Command. Some of them are: how to maintain and exercise a nucleus force to provide an instant response to a contingency, how to apportion DOD cargo between its own and commercial carriers, and how to fulfill its defined mission in the face of tighter DOD budgets. Some of these have already been addressed in detail, but one not yet considered is: How will DOD apportion its decreasing total peacetime cargo movement between sealift and airlift?

---

[33] Ibid.

6

THE MILITARY TRAFFIC MANAGEMENT COMMAND

The Military Traffic Management Command is descended from the Defense Traffic Management Service and the Military Traffic Management and Terminal Service. MTMC is one of three DOD single-manager Transportation Operating Agencies, the others being the Military Airlift Command and the Military Sealift Command. The commanding general of MTMC is the executive agent for the secretary of the army, the DOD's single manager responsible for ocean terminal service and land transportation in the continental United States. In 1973, the command employed approximately 5,700 civilians, 1,400 contract stevedores, and 900 military personnel.[1] By 1975, personnel in all groups had been reduced considerably because of the American disengagement from Vietnam and the greater use of civilian ports and terminals.

MTMC's terminal management operations are industrially funded, that is, the military customer pays MTMC for the service rendered. The extent of this operation is indicated by the agency's industrial fund: in 1974 it amounted to $139.3 million, in 1975 an estimated $144.5 million, and in 1976 an estimated $155.2 million.[2] Traffic management functions are funded by the Department of the Army.

MTMC differs from MAC and MSC in two respects. First, it is the only one that is jointly staffed by the navy and air force. Second, MTMC does not operate a complete transportation system, as does MAC with its airline and MSC with its shipping firm, but has relied instead on commercial transportation assets.

---

[1] Eston T. White, *Transportation* (Washington, D.C.: Industrial College of the Armed Forces, 1974), p. 123.

[2] *The Budget of the United States Government 1976*, p. 333.

MTMC's Mission

In essence, MTMC is the traffic manager for the Department of Defense, dealing with commercial carriers as well as MAC and MSC.[3] It manages the worldwide movement and storage of DOD household goods, provides ocean terminal service in the United States, and has responsibility for overseas army terminal units. MTMC is also charged with developing strategic movement plans for the joint chiefs of staff in time of mobilization, and it plans for the efficient day-to-day use of military and commercial land transportation in the United States. The command advises DOD of the impact of various railroad reorganization plans on defense requirements. It is DOD's executive agent in the highways-for-national-defense program, and it administers the Military Standard Transportation and Movement Procedures (MILSTAMP) program, which was developed to keep the management of DOD cargo movement, particularly freight documentation, abreast of the latest commercial technology.

As the DOD traffic manager, MTMC routinely deals with the commercial transportation world. In fiscal year 1974, DOD shipped approximately 40 million short tons of cargo at a cost of $3.5 billion, most of it by commercial carriers.

Railroads. DOD peacetime railroad operations, including the movement of cargo and passengers, can be compared with commercial operations in the following statistics. In 1974, U.S. commercial railroads originated 1.54 billion tons of freight, carried 274 million passengers (including both commuters and intercity passengers), and owned 1.4 million railroad cars, of which 3,333 were tank cars.[4]

In FY 1974, in the continental United States, railroads carried 3.7 million tons of DOD freight (of a DOD total of 17 million tons of freight) and transported 100,000 DOD passengers (of a DOD total of 5 million). DOD owned 4,149 rail cars, of which 2,287 were tank cars.[5]

---

[3] MTMC must also have a detailed understanding of the purpose and authority of the regulatory commissions, such as the Interstate Commerce Commission, the Federal Maritime Board, and the Civil Aeronautics Board. The agency also coordinated DOD interests with respect to quasi-public transportation companies such as the National Rail Passenger Corporation (AMTRAK). In the past MTMC has made available to AMTRAK DOD-owned railroad passenger cars and has encouraged AMTRAK to submit tenders of service for bulk passenger movements.

[4] *Yearbook of Railroad Facts: 1975* (Washington, D.C.: Economics and Finance Department, Association of American Railroads, 1975), pp. 13, 14, 28, 30, 48, 52, and 54.

[5] *The Official Railway Equipment Register*, April 1975, p. 769. The Department of Defense does not operate any rail passenger cars and its owned tracks are limited to those found on military installations.

In summary, DOD cargo and passenger movement accounted for about 0.24 percent and 0.036 percent respectively of the total U.S. rail cargo and passenger movement, but railroads carried about 22 percent of total DOD freight. In a mobilization or war, this share could be expected to increase substantially. The Department of Defense must rely to a significant extent on the nation's railroads for movement in the continental United States, but DOD business accounts for only a small proportion of rail revenues.

The Defense Freight Railway Interchange Fleet (DFRIF). As noted, the Department of Defense does own railroad rolling stock, and MTMC is the agency charged with managing it, but not in the manner that MAC and MSC operate airlines and shipping services. All transportation systems may be said to comprise two components—the path and the vehicle. All three agencies, MAC, MSC, and MTMC, operate vehicles, but only MAC and MSC control the paths these vehicles use. MAC operates its own aerial ports and utilizes publicly owned or international airlanes, and, in the same way, MSC utilizes publicly owned ports and international sealanes. Although MTMC operates railroad rolling stock, it must rely on a privately owned path. MTMC is in the same category as any nonrailroad corporation that owns rail cars, such as the large oil companies.

DOD investment in railroad rolling stock was once considerably greater than it is today, and, as in sea and land transportation, there was once a significant duplication of effort. The Hoover Commission Task Force on Transportation found that in 1955 the army owned 4,728 rail cars of all types, and the navy, 2,580. In 1956, when the secretary of the army assumed management of land transportation in the continental United States, most DOD-owned railroad rolling stock was transferred to the army.

In 1975, the MTMC-operated DFRIF fleet was composed of:

$$
\begin{array}{lr}
\text{Box cars} & 927 \\
\text{Flat cars} & 934 \\
\text{Tank cars} & 2287 \\
\text{Gondolas} & 1 \\
\hline
& 4149 \text{ [6]}
\end{array}
$$

DOD's investment in railroad stock is relatively small when compared with that of private companies. In 1975, the Southern Railway Company owned 75,638 freight and 49 tank cars, and the Union

---

[6] *The Official Railway Equipment Register,* pp. 768–769.

Pacific Railroad owned 68,744 freight cars and 562 tank cars.[7] In its FY 1974 budget, DOD requested funds to purchase 750 railway tank cars of 20,000-gallon capacity. These cars were to replace, on a one-for-two basis, the older DFRIF 10,000-gallon cars. This fleet would service the petroleum product requirements of all defense installations in the continental United States, which total eight million barrels a year.[8] The DOD boxcar and flat car fleet is also aging, however, and will have to be replaced, or the cars will have to be leased from the commercial sector.[9]

In evaluating the need for DOD-owned railroad rolling stock, it should be noted that major railroads have very little invested in tank cars. A mere 49 tank cars are owned by the Southern and the 562 by Union Pacific—far fewer than their freight car inventories. Most tank cars are owned by the major oil companies, hence the DOD tank car fleet does not duplicate a railroad capability, though it might duplicate an oil company service. No oil company, however, has ever objected to the DFRIF fleet.

The presumption of a DOD need for freight cars is not as strong as for tank cars. During the 1974–75 recession, the nation's railroads laid up tens of thousands of cars. The Southern set aside and stored 7,600 freight cars.[10] Thus, before replacing the freight car portion of the DFRIF fleet, DOD should demonstrate that in peacetime privately owned railroads cannot fulfill defense freight car needs and, in a nonmobilization contingency, the needed railroad rolling stock cannot be rapidly acquired.

Highways. In the United States, use of military motor transportation is limited to training, local administrative movement, and meeting emergency requirements. Such activity is generally confined to mili-

---

[7] Ibid., pp. 630–631, 669.

[8] In a letter report to the secretary of the army, the U.S. General Accounting Office questioned the need for the 750 car order, citing a declining movement of DOD petroleum products. However, it did not question the DOD prerogative of maintaining a DFRIF fleet. See Comptroller General of the United States, *Letter Report B-182033* (Washington, D.C.: U.S. General Accounting Office, 1974). When commercial rail carriers use cars in the DFRIF fleet, DOD is paid for this use in exactly the same way that such charges are assessed among privately owned companies.

[9] During the Korean War, the army purchased approximately 3,700 rail freight cars for contingency use in Europe. More than 600 were placed in service, and the remainder stored, never having been used. In 1973, the cost of retaining this stored fleet was about $500,000 annually. Whether some of this rolling stock could be made serviceable is highly problematical. Most are stored in a knock-down condition and would require extensive overhauls. Most likely, the army will decide to scrap them.

[10] Southern Railway Company, *Stockholder's Newsletter*, March 1975.

tary installations and the immediate surrounding area. Thus, the MTMC function in highway transportation is largely coordinative. As DOD's traffic manager, it contracts needed commercial motor transport service (approximately $117 million in FY 1974) and directs the DOD Highways for National Defense Program, evaluating highway programs for defense requirements and making recommendations to the secretary of transportation and other agencies. MTMC also authorizes construction of access roads to defense installations, initiates traffic engineering studies of existing roads, and acts as the DOD representative in discussions with state and federal highway officials regarding highway design, bridge clearances, weight limits— all to insure that the nation's highways will serve military needs effectively.

Military Ocean Terminals. MTMC owns and operates three ocean terminals in the United States, at Bayonne, N.J.; Oakland, Calif.; and Sunny Point, N.C., and owns an inactive terminal at Kings Bay, Ga. In addition to its own terminals, MTMC moves cargo through certain commercial terminals, designated outports which have MTMC personnel assigned to them. They are located at Seattle, Wash.; North Charleston, S.C.; New Orleans, La.; Beaumont, Tex.; Mobile, Ala.; Long Beach, Calif.; Baltimore, Md.; Philadelphia, Pa.; and Cape Canaveral, Fla.[11] MTMC also operates a number of Military Terminal Units in foreign countries. The Bayonne and Oakland terminals are most relevant to consideration of full utilization of commercial facilities. Sunny Point, N.C., is used exclusively for ammunition movement, as would be Kings Bay, Ga., if it were reactivated. MTMC has already adopted the position that commercial facilities should be fully used, even if competing military facilities must be closed. Major General H. R. Del Mar, commander of MTMC, said:

> The Bayonne and Oakland terminals have been outmoded by transportation distribution technology and are increasingly underutilized. The advent of containerization has had a tremendous impact on DOD and commercial cargo transportation, with many commercial facilities converting to or adding container handling equipment.
>
> In 1970, MTMC elected to move DOD container cargo through commercial container facilities on the east and west coasts, rather than install duplicate facilities at the Bayonne

---

[11] When requested, the navy will provide MTMC with common-user ocean terminal service under an interservice support agreement. Likewise, MTMC will service navy requirements at its Oakland, Calif., and Bayonne, N.J., terminals. Whether the navy could use commercial facilities in a fleet-support role in lieu of its own terminals—though a fair question—is beyond the scope of this study.

and Oakland terminals. The commercial facilities can meet DOD contingency and support requirements.[12]

The transfer of all work from Bayonne and Oakland was scheduled for completion in 1977 without a decision on whether these terminals would be mothballed or declared excess. Nor is there unanimous agreement within DOD about relying completely on commercial facilities. Opponents say Military Ocean Terminals are more secure and less likely to be shut down by labor disputes. In rebuttal, MTMC officials point out that a longshoremen's strike can close down a military ocean terminal as easily as a commercial one.

The move toward MTMC's complete reliance upon commercial terminal facilities is sound, the more so given the decline in DOD overseas shipments from a high of 28 million measurement tons in 1968 to less than half that amount in 1975. Considerable savings can be expected as DOD cargo becomes a part of the high-volume operations of commercial terminals.

Container Service. In 1975, the U.S. container inventory was estimated to be in excess of 750,000 twenty-foot eight-by-eight equivalent containers. At the same time, the DOD inventory was approximately 6,700 military containers (MILVANS) of this size, and 5,600 chassis. During the Vietnam War, it was proposed that DOD acquire a container distribution system ostensibly to offer service in areas not served by commercial firms.[13] Ultimately, the system would have included containers, chassis, supporting hardware, and container terminals. With the drawdown of American forces in Vietnam, however, along with the consequent tightening of defense budgets and the MTMC decision not to equip military ocean terminals with container cranes, the container distribution system was shelved. One exception to MTMC's almost complete reliance on the commercial sector is the movement of ammunition in MILVANS. Relatively few commercial containers are certified by the American Association of Railroads or the Coast Guard for this use, though extensive attempts were made to adapt commercial containers for this purpose. No agency in DOD has control over the complete MILVAN system. The Army Material Com-

---

[12] H. R. Del Mar, "Streamlining for Tomorrow," *Defense Management Journal,* vol. 11 (April 1975), p. 33.

[13] A second justification was that many of the older and smaller CONEX (Container Express) military containers required replacement. Of an original inventory of 200,000, about 75,000 CONEXs were still in service, mostly being used for storage. In time, the CONEX will be dropped from the DOD inventory. For a good description of the CONEX system in a wartime environment, see Frank S. Besson, Jr., "CONEX: Logistics Wonder-Worker in Vietnam," *National Defense Transportation Journal,* June 1966.

mand owns most of the containers, and management is fragmented between MTMC, the Military Sealift Command, and the overseas military commands. With an increasing percentage of military cargo moving in containers, the Department of Defense in 1973 established a project manager to develop a surface container distribution system throughout DOD. The primary mission of this group was to insure that DOD requirements could be met and were compatible with the commercial system. Under the project manager concept, a number of problems were explored and some solutions gained. The charter for this project, however, terminated on July 1, 1975, and research efforts were farmed out to the services.[14] DOD's container management is now focused more on MTMC than any other agency, mainly because the DOD shippers want door-to-door service, that is, to load the container at inland points in the continental United States and have it moved straight through to an overseas destination. Since MTMC is the agency responsible for management of inland transportation in the continental United States, it is reasonable to consider the agency as the de facto manager in this respect.

Air, Water, and Pipelines. The Department of Defense operates neither inland waterway transportation systems nor pipelines,[15] but these systems are scarcely neglected in defense planning. In World War II, both inland waterways and pipelines were extremely important to the nation's mobilization. Pipelines offered an alternative to the movement of petroleum products along the coast by tankers, which suffered heavy losses from submarines in the early years of the war. MTMC plans maximum use of these systems during a mobilization.

Although the services generally accept MTMC's management of DOD requirements for inland waterways and pipelines, there is considerably less agreement on the agency's role in the military air cargo management. In 1968, MTMC's predecessor, the Military Traffic Management and Terminal Service, established the Military Air Clearance Authority Agency (MACAA) to control the movement of cargo into the military airlift system. In a 1973 assessment of MTMC's military air cargo function, the General Accounting Office found duplication

---

[14] The DOD-wide surface container distribution system is discussed more fully in Chapter 7.

[15] DOD might be said to provide the "path" component of the inland water transportation system because the Corps of Engineers has the primary responsibility for maintaining the navigable river system in the United States. Both the army and the navy maintain a number of small watercraft on the harbor and river system. Included are tugs, barges of different types, utility boats, ferries, lighters, and various kinds of service craft.

by MTMC and the Shipper Service Control Offices of the army, navy, and air force. According to the GAO report, the military departments contended each service must control its own cargo and was reluctant to accept MTMC as a single manager for air export cargo.

In 1971, the air force proposed that MACAA be disestablished and its functions be assumed by the air force. In 1972, MTMTS (MTMC) proposed a reorganization of MACAA and the shipper service control offices to eliminate duplication and make the best use of the resources of all services. In its report to the secretary of defense, GAO concluded: "MTMTS [MTMC] has never functioned as an effective single manager for air export cargo because of opposition from the services and the lack of support from the office of the Secretary of Defense. The de facto division of management authority has led to duplicated efforts."[16]

The report indicated where more efficient operations would be achieved with MTMC as the single management authority. The final GAO recommendation was:

> We recommend that the Secretary of Defense (1) enforce and augment, as necessary, DOD Directive 5160.53 which establishes MTMTS as a single manager for air export cargo and (2) prohibit other service elements from duplicating MACAA functions. Considering the advantages to be derived and the work already done by MTMTS in this area, we further recommend that this action include consideration of MTMTS' reorganization proposal.[17]

The annual potential saving to DOD if MTMC were recognized as the single manager for air export cargo was estimated to be $1.5 million.[18]

The Problem of Section 22 Rates

A major responsibility of MTMC is to obtain good transportation service from commercial carriers at reasonable rates. When rates or service are considered unreasonable, MTMC tries to obtain relief or reimbursement. Under the Armed Services Procurement Act, government agencies must procure goods and services at the lowest possible

---

[16] Comptroller General of the United States, *Letter Report B-133025* (Washington, D.C.: U.S. General Accounting Office, 1973), p. 7.

[17] Ibid., p. 8.

[18] In July 1975, the MACAA was disestablished. Its export airlift clearance function was transferred to the Shipper Service Control Offices and to the Military Airlift Command.

price. Although procurement of much transportation service is exempt from the act, MTMC negotiates with private carriers with price in mind, and it is greatly aided by Section 22 of the original Act to Regulate Commerce passed in 1887, which allows carriers to make "rate concessions" to the federal government. These rates are exempt from ICC regulation. Section 22 says:

> That nothing in this act shall apply to the carriage, storage, or handling of property free or at reduced rates for the United States, State or municipal governments, or for charitable purposes or to or from fairs and expositions for exhibition thereat, or the issuance of mileage, excursion, or commutation passenger tickets; nothing in this act shall be construed to prohibit any common carrier from giving reduced rates to ministers of religion; nothing in this act shall be construed to prevent railroads from giving free carriage to their own officers and employees, or to prevent the principal officers of any railroad company or companies from exchanging passes or tickets with other railroad companies for their officers and employees; and nothing in this act contained shall in any way abridge or alter the remedies now existing at common law or by statute, but the provisions of this act are in addition to such remedies: Provided, that no pending litigation shall in any way be affected by this act.[19]

Prior to 1887, much government and military traffic moved at so-called land grant rates—rate concessions made partly in return for large tracts of land granted to the railroads between 1850 and 1870. About 130 million acres were given, primarily to encourage westward expansion of railroads. During the nineteenth century the federal government was only a nominal user of transportation services, and Section 22 rates had little impact on carrier revenues. In World War I, however, all of this changed, and since the end of World War II the federal government—particularly DOD—has been a significant user of commercial transportation. In 1946, land grant rates were repealed, leaving only Section 22 as the basis for the government to seek rate concessions from commercial carriers. Since that time, a number of carriers, transportation associations, and shippers have sought to repeal Section 22 or, failing that, to limit it to times of war or mobilization. The proposed Surface Transportation Act of 1973 included a provision that would have required Section 22 rates not be less than the variable costs of handling such traffic. Later, the proposed Transportation Improvement Act of 1974 contained a provision (Section 7) that would limit Section 22 rates to time of war and to the transporta-

---

[19] Act to Regulate Commerce of 1887, in *U.S. Statutes at Large*, vol. 24, p. 387.

tion of bulk and agricultural commodities. In December 1974, the House passed a revised Surface Transportation Act, but prior to the vote, the provision to repeal Section 22 was deleted. In arguing for retention of Section 22, Representative F. Edward Hebert (Democrat, Louisiana), chairman of the House Armed Services Committee, and Representative George H. Mahon (Democrat, Texas), chairman of the House Appropriations Committee, estimated that DOD saved $250 million a year by negotiating freight charges instead of using the commercial tariff rate structure. The House bill, H.R. 5385, was tabled by a unanimous vote of the Senate Commerce Committee on December 17, 1974.

The Case for Section 22. The justification for retaining Section 22 is the savings realized by DOD. The U.S. General Accounting Office reviewed Section 22 rates and concluded that charges under the section were compensatory whether fully allocated or variable costs were used. It also concluded that significant savings, in fact, were achieved by DOD:

> On the basis of an analysis of a statistical sample, we estimate that in the 7 month period (May–November 1972) the Government shipped about 5.3 billion pounds of rail carload freight and paid related line-haul transportation charges totaling about $80.8 million at rates under Section 22. These shipments constituted 77 percent of the total carload weight shipped during this period and 81 percent of the related line-haul charges. On the basis of rail carload cost scales published by the Interstate Commerce Commission, we estimate that the carriers' fully allocated costs of transporting the 5.3 billion pounds were about $37.2 million and the variable costs were about $29.4 million. The charges paid under Section 22 were $43.6 million above carriers' fully allocated costs and $51.4 million above carriers' variable costs.
>
> Had payment for these Section 22 shipments been made on the basis of available tariffs, the cost to the Government would have been increased by about $105.6 million. The tariff charges, however, were $149.2 million above carriers' fully allocated costs and $157 million above carriers' variable costs.[20]

In its review of truck freight, GAO concluded:

> Our sample of shipments for the 7 month period (May–November 1972) showed that the Government . . . shipped

[20] Comptroller General of the United States, *Letter Report B-177692* (Washington, D.C.: U.S. General Accounting Office, 1974), pp. 1–2.

motor truckload freight weighing about 3 billion pounds at rates under Section 22, which was 71 percent of all such weight shipped by the Department of Defense during this period, and . . . paid line haul charges of about $60.1 million at rates under Section 22, which amounted to 78 percent of all such charges paid by the Department on truckload freight.[21]

The motor carriers' fully allocated costs of hauling the 3 billion pounds were about $55.3 million. Thus, the overall section charges were $4.8 million more than carriers' fully allocated costs. If Section 22 were not available, the government would have had to pay the motor carriers an additional $36.6 million to move its traffic at tariff rates. These tariff charges were about $41.4 million more than the carriers' costs.

Those favoring retention of Section 22 say military traffic charged under this section moves under rates published in some 20,000 tenders, of which approximately 900 are negotiated, and that the tendered rates are voluntarily submitted by the carriers. Moreover, it is argued, Section 22 allows DOD to negotiate commodity rates when it would otherwise be charged class rates.

> Most volume shippers' commercial traffic moves on commodity rates, while low volume or irregular traffic moves on higher class rates. When DOD makes a volume shipment of a commodity to a point for which no commercial rate exists, the applicable rate would be a high class rate, even though the same shipment moving to a nearby point might be eligible for a lower commodity rate.
>
> In such cases, either DOD can request a rate adjustment from a carrier . . . or the carrier may offer such a rate. This adjusted rate, generally Section 22 for the reasons stated earlier, would be lower than the existing class rate and would normally be based on the commodity rates which apply to similar commodities moving under similar conditions. This is how a Section 22 rate can be a reduction from an existing rate (the class rate) but be nevertheless profitable and comparable to another existing commodity rate.[22]

DOD traffic, as noted earlier, accounts for only a small percentage of commercial carrier revenues, hence the impact on carriers of a Section 22 rate concession is minimal.

---

[21] Comptroller General of the United States, *Letter Report B-177692* (Washington, D.C.: U.S. General Accounting Office, 1975), pp. 1–2.

[22] Ezio Balducci, "The Sad Misunderstanding of Section 22," *Translog: Journal of the Military Transportation Management Command*, November–December 1974, pp. 6–7.

The Case Against Section 22. The argument for repeal of Section 22 rests on two grounds: first, the private shipper, in effect, subsidizes DOD cargo, and, second, rate concessions to DOD further imperil an already financially shaky U.S. transportation system. These arguments have been urged upon Congress by all elements of the U.S. surface transportation industry.[23]

Although the impact of negotiated rates on total carrier revenues may indeed be small, the relevant test of Section 22 is best seen by an examination of business decision making at the margin *and* in a consideration of alternate uses, in both hardware and capital expenditures, of DOD's estimated $250 million annual saving.

DOD spokesmen have continually stressed the necessity of a viable U.S. commercial transportation system. They argue that an efficient commercial system must be in place should a war or mobilization occur. A viable transportation service is achieved, however, by day-by-day decisions to invest funds in the system. A decision to expand a particular service in the short run, for example, will be based on an expected increase in revenues. Even a small increase may bring forth an expansion of service or make a current service more secure. A decision on how much transportation service to offer in the long run will also depend upon the anticipated return on investment. DOD's $250 million annual "savings" must be considered in this respect. How would the U.S. transportation system benefit from this amount? Consider these data. (1) The Transportation Act of 1958 provided that the federal government would guarantee over a period of fifteen years a total of $500 million in loans to railroads to be used for capital and maintenance expenditures. (2) The original grant to finance the National Railroad Passenger Corporation in 1970 was $200 million. (3) In 1971 the cost of continuing development of an American commercial supersonic transport (SST) plane was $290 million. (4) In late 1975, the House passed the so-called Railroad Jobs bill (H.R. 8672), which would make available $240 million in grants, for labor costs only, to rehabilitate railroad beds in the Northeast. The point is that the $250 million annual DOD savings could be used in a number of ways to improve the overall U.S. transportation system. While there

---

[23] The Interstate Commerce Commission also favors limiting Section 22 to times of war and to the transportation of bulk and agricultural commodities. This book does not address the claim that DOD, by using its prerogative to negotiate rates, is in effect being subsidized by the private sector. Testimony and data in this respect—both pro and con—are voluminous, and the reader is referred to the relevant congressional hearings. Even if the subsidy charge were disproved (and this is by no means certain), the correct question is still, Should DOD, as one of the nation's largest shippers, use its economic and legal (Section 22) power to achieve the lowest possible transportation charge for the movement of military cargo?

is no guarantee that transportation firms would use additional revenues from DOD traffic in these ways, most of them would probably go for capital improvements and maintenance expenditures. Railroad aid bills under consideration by Congress call for several billions of dollars in low-interest loans for roadbed repairs and equipment acquisition.

Now consider what military purchases DOD could make with its transportation savings. Based on 1974 estimates, $250 million would buy either 3 B-1 intercontinental bombers, ⅙ of a Trident submarine, approximately 240 XM1 main battle tanks, or 15 F-15 fighter aircraft.[24] It is not suggested that these buys are unimportant, but they should be weighed against DOD's requirement of a viable and efficient U.S. transport system. In reality, however, this is not a decision for DOD to make, but rather for the executive branch and ultimately Congress. Assuming funds will be made available one way or another, the essential question is, What is the most efficient way to get additional federal funds into the transportation system? It makes little sense to rob Peter and pay Paul, that is, on the one hand to achieve a "savings" at DOD and on the other to increase outlays by another federal agency, the Department of Transportation, to improve the nation's transportation system. Congress should be aware that if the above view is accepted, no saving in overall federal spending is taking place.

Other Problems. Since DOD, through MTMC, relies primarily upon the private sector for surface transportation in the continental United States, it must face the same problems that beset the commercial shipper. Among the more important of these problems are rapidly increasing transportation costs at a time when the DOD dollar is shrinking in purchasing power, shortages of equipment, deteriorating service, and the possibility of an interruption of transportation by strikes and labor disputes.

In remarks delivered on March 12, 1975, before a National Defense Transportation Association seminar, Major General H. R. Del Mar, the commanding general of MTMC, noted the deterioration of transportation service:

> Recently, there appears to be an increasing urge to sweep our failures and shortcomings beneath the skirts of inflation, the energy crisis, spiraling costs of operation and reduced workforce ... I contend that a major contributing factor to industry's increased operating ratios and decreased rate of

---

[24] Comptroller General of the United States, *Status of Selected Major Weapon Systems* (Washington, D.C.: U.S. General Accounting Office, 1975), Appendix 3, p. 20.

return on investment is not inflation . . . but rather inadequate controls and ineffective traffic management. Likewise, the rise in costs is no excuse for degradation of service. Nonetheless, the trend in providing satisfactory service has sharply decreased, while the price DOD pays for service has sharply increased. The first half of fiscal year 75 showed a 20 percent decrease in the number of personal property shipments made for our military members. However, overall costs increased 8 percent. The average cost per shipment rose 28 percent domestically and 23 percent internationally. Unfortunately a corresponding increase in the quality of service has not been realized. In fiscal year 1972, 83 percent of domestic shipments were delivered on time. This decreased to 77 percent in fiscal year 1973, and to 75 percent in fiscal year 1974. Likewise, international on-time deliveries amounted to 72 percent in 1972, 53 percent in 1973 . . . and to a low 44 percent in 1974.

Another major problem facing MTMC is a shortage of containers for military cargo, as occurred in late 1973 and the first part of 1974. The shortfall was attributed to several factors: an increased demand for American products following devaluation with a consequent increased demand for containers, work stoppages and slowdowns by truckers protesting lower speed limits and gasoline shortages, and efforts of steamship operators to save fuel by slowing down their vessels. Secondary factors contributing to the shortage were the phaseout of twenty-foot containers (which were not replaced) by commercial operators, and the reluctance of shipping firms to forgo commercial cargo in order to move lower-valued DOD cargo. Colonel Mark L. Maloney, chief of the Overseas Cargo Division of MTMC, summarized the shortfall:

> Among the lessons learned from the container crisis was the vulnerability of the system of shipping Department of Defense cargo via commercial container carriers. The Department had come to depend heavily on a system that proved to lack responsiveness.
>
> Would the next shortfall be of longer duration, cause greater backlogs, and lead to a complete breakdown of our logistics pipeline? Would container ships be readily available for charter during a future shortfall? Will sufficient military containers be available, and *could or should an increase in their inventory be justified* [italics supplied]? Are greater commitments by ocean carriers needed in current and future container agreements to provide containers where and when needed by the Department of Defense? Are such commit-

ments possible in view of the fact that, by law, ocean carriers are also common carriers and must be responsive to commercial as well as Defense Department shippers? These are only a few of the serious questions raised.[25]

Conclusion

MTMC is closer than either MSC or MAC to the commercial transportation sector. As DOD's traffic manager, it is in the best position to match DOD requirements efficiently to commercial capabilities on land, sea, and air, both in the continental United States and overseas. Three problems, however, remain unresolved. One is a resolution of the Section 22 controversy. At present, it is an irritant in relations with the private transportation sector, and it could become worse. In this respect, it must be determined whether the end result of lower transport charges for DOD is worth the price paid, particularly when it is realized that any DOD payment can also be viewed as a DOD investment in a viable U.S. transportation system.[26]

A second problem is the failure of DOD and its several services to accept a single DOD traffic manager in the continental United States. Procrastination has been allowed to continue at considerable expense, as the General Accounting Office has pointed out.

A final problem is the management and movement of military cargo in an increasingly containerized world. The container shortfall of 1974 did not prove, in any sense, Colonel Maloney's contention that the commercial system lacked responsiveness, but it did pinpoint a potential problem area.

---

[25] Mark L. Maloney, "Container Crisis," *Army Logistician*, vol. 7 (January–February 1975), p. 32 (unpublished).

[26] Section 207 of the recently passed Railroad Revitalization and Regulatory Reform Act (Public Law 94-210, 94th Cong., S. 2718) grants the Interstate Commerce Commission, upon petition and after hearings, authority to exempt certain classes of limited traffic that would not affect the goal of achieving a viable national rail transportation system. Similarly the commission may also revoke any exemption granted. Whether this legislation will mitigate to any significant extent the Section 22 controversy remains to be seen.

7
INTERMODAL
TRANSPORTATION

This chapter examines the way in which the Department of Defense as a shipper of cargo interfaces with the commercial U.S. intermodal transportation system. Problems arise because a number of DOD transportation requirements have no commercial counterpart but must be solved within the constraints of the commercial system. A number of these problems become extremely critical in a wartime environment.

Intermodal transportation can be defined simply as "the transfer of freight vehicles or their load carrying structure between two or more modes of travel."[1] Examples of the first include truck trailers carried on railroad flat cars, the so-called "piggyback" system, and truck and railroad cars carried on ships. In these instances, the vehicles themselves are transported. In the second case, the load-carrying structures are transferred between modes. The primary example is the movement of standard-size containers from and to trucks, trains, ships and planes.

Containers

Containers come in a variety of sizes and configurations. Most are eight feet by eight feet, with lengths ranging from twenty feet to forty feet. The most common lengths are twenty, thirty-five, and forty feet. The enclosed dry van type of container accounts for over 95 percent of the U.S. container inventory.[2]

---

[1] Benton H. Elliott and Philip S. Noble, "Intermodal Transportation Systems," *Proceedings, Intersociety Conference on Transportation* (New York: Society of Automotive Engineers, 1972), p. 40.

[2] Other major container types include the refrigerated container, the insulated container, the open-top and open-side container, and the flat rack, essentially an open-top and open-side container.

In 1959, the total number of containers in the United States was 138,000, of which 80,000 were of the military CONEX type.[3] In 1974, the U.S. inventory of twenty-foot equivalents totaled 697,000, excluding CONEX containers. In 1976, the total U.S. container inventory probably exceeds 800,000, excluding approximately 6,700 military containers (MILVANS) and 75,000 of the smaller CONEX containers in the DOD inventory.

The Department of Defense elected to rely primarily upon commercial containers and is now shipping about 80 percent of its overseas cargo in containers, almost all in commercial containers. Thus, the U.S. commercial container distribution system has become critical to DOD peacetime cargo movement and to contingency planning.[4]

The U.S. Intermodal Transportation System

Contrary to popular belief, intermodal transportation is not new. Ferries, for example, have been available a long time. A more significant example was the Pennsylvania Public Works, completed in 1834, an intermodal system connecting Philadelphia and Pittsburgh by a system of canals and railroads. Carrying structures were canal barges built in sections. In movements by rail, usually over areas where it was not feasible to construct a canal, barge sections were mounted on flat cars and carried to the next canal. The Pennsylvania Public Works system was not cost-effective, however, when competing with the all-water Erie Canal and, later, with all-rail routes.[5] Parts of the system were gradually abandoned, and by the end of the nineteenth century this early intermodal system had largely passed into history.

Following World War II, several economic factors combined to create a favorable environment for intermodal transportation. One factor was the rapid increase in labor costs, particularly stevedoring, and another was the explosive growth in world trade, with an at-

---

[3] John G. Shott, *Progress in Piggyback and Containerization* (Washington, D.C.: Public Affairs Institute, 1961), p. 11. CONEX ("Container Express") is a steel container that comes in two sizes: four feet by six feet by six feet, and eight feet by six feet by six feet. The concept was developed by the army's Transportation Corps and was first used during the Korean War. Cargo handling was facilitated (the CONEX could be easily stowed and transported), there was less damage and pilferage, and delivery time was reduced markedly.

[4] J.J. Morris, "Containers: Their Role in Military Distribution," *Defense Transportation Journal*, vol. 30 (June 1975), p. 13.

[5] The cost of the main line of the Pennsylvania Public Works was $10 million, a substantially greater sum at that time than now. For a brief description of the system, see Locklin, *Economics of Transportation*, pp. 97–99.

tendant demand for faster and more economical service. A third factor was cargo security: in the 1950s, losses from cargo pilferage were estimated in the billions of dollars. A load-carrying structure that could be easily transferred from one transport mode to another without the necessity of breaking down and transferring cargo offered at least partial solutions to many problems. In the mid-1970s, with the inauguration of container air service—though limited—the commercial container distribution system became truly intermodal.

The Ocean Systems. In the three ocean intermodal systems, the associated carriers are the containership, the roll on/roll off vessel (RO/RO), and the lighter aboard ship (LASH) or the seabarge (SEABEE) ship. In the containership system, cargo is loaded ("stuffed") into a standard-size container at an inland point of origin—usually the shipper's warehouse or plant—then moved by rail or truck to an ocean terminal, loaded aboard a containership for movement to an overseas destination, unloaded at a container terminal, and eventually loaded on a land carrier for delivery to its ultimate destination. Components of the system include the container, the containership, and the containerport, which includes a rail terminal, special container cranes for vessel loading, a large container storage area, container handling equipment, and one or more land carriers to move the containers to and from the containerport. In this system, containers may be either loaded directly onto the land carrier (a truck or a rail car) or deposited in the storage area or at the rail terminal for later loading or unloading at dockside.

In the roll on/roll off mode, the cargo is loaded aboard a vehicle at an inland point, transported to the RO/RO pier, and driven aboard the RO/RO ship. Upon arrival in port, the vehicle is driven off the ship and moves out to its destination. Components of the system include the RO/RO ship, a relatively simple loading pier, a small storage area, and the wheeled vehicle, which may be either the cab and trailer or the trailer alone.

In the LASH and SEABEE system, cargo (including containers on the larger barges) is loaded onto lighters or barges at inland points on navigable rivers and moved to the LASH or SEABEE vessel.[6] The ship is equipped to lift and stow the lighter or barge aboard. At its overseas destination, the lighter or barge is unloaded and moved to its inland destination. System components include the vessel, the barge or lighter, standard piers, and standard port cargo handling equipment.

---

[6] In addition to economically marrying the ocean system to the inland waterway system, the LASH and SEABEE systems are efficient methods of loading and discharging cargo at ports lacking piers and warehousing.

The Land Systems. The land intermodal system is composed of railroads that can transport either containers or vehicles and the associated highway carrier. Generally, the railroad moves cargo over the long leg of the journey, and the highway carrier transports the container or trailer from the point of origin to the rail terminal and, at the end of the rail journey, from the terminal to the final destination. Components of the system include the container or wheeled trailer, the highway carrier, the rail carrier, a container rail terminal (including a large area set aside for container storage), and specialized container-handling equipment.

The Air System. The air intermodal system is still in its infancy, but it merits mention. The primary carriers are the Boeing 747F and the newly announced McDonnell Douglas DC-10-30AF all freight carrier. Cargo is loaded in a standard container and moved to the airport by a highway carrier, where it is loaded aboard the airplane for the overseas or long leg of its trip. On arrival at the airport, it is unloaded onto a highway carrier for delivery to the final destination. Components of the system are the standard container, the airplane, the air freight terminal, and special container-handling equipment for loading and unloading the airplane.

Problems in the Ocean, Land, and Air Systems

Intermodal transportation systems that DOD must rely upon as a shipper of cargo have been briefly described, and the major problems that DOD faces in utilizing the system will now be examined. Particular attention will be given to how DOD interfaces with the commercial container distribution system in achieving a DOD container distribution system.

Ocean System Problems. The decline of the break-bulk component of the American merchant marine deprived Pentagon planners of the versatility of a ship that could load and unload with its own gear, accept outsize cargo (that is, cargo that cannot be containerized), and transport ammunition. Of the three ocean intermodal systems—containerships, RO/ROs, and LASH and SEABEE—the containership presents the greatest problem for contingency planning.[7]

---

[7] In 1975 there were twelve RO/RO and twenty-three LASH/SEABEE ships in the general cargo fleet of 307 vessels. These versatile ships fit well into Pentagon contingency planning. The RO/RO can transport wheeled vehicles and tanks, while the horizontal-loading SEABEE can transport non-self-deployable aircraft. But the RO/RO requires lighters and a deepwater pier to discharge its cargo, and seabarges require some docking facility and cranes to unload heavy equipment.

Containerships are either self-sustaining, that is, able to load and unload their own containers, or non-self-sustaining, and dependent upon expensive and complex shoreside facilities to load and discharge. In 1975, there were 21 self-sustaining and 92 non-self-sustaining containerships in the American-flag fleet. By 1985, there will be an estimated 130 U.S.-flag non-self-sustaining containerships, approximately 50 percent of the general cargo fleet.

Containership problem areas include the following:

How can a non-self-sustaining containership be discharged when there are no shore facilities available? Offshore discharge of containerships is a problem of particular concern in a wartime environment, when container ports might be denied because of enemy action, or when containerships might be needed to support an across-the-shore landing where there was no container port to begin with.[8]

How can the non-self-sustaining containership be used in an underway replenishment role? With the increase of containerships in the U.S. inventory, this type of ship might be all that is available to the navy for underway replenishment in wartime. In 1969, the Office of Naval Research contracted with the National Academy of Sciences to evaluate the use of containerships in this way.[9] Work in the area is ongoing. The navy's Merchant Ship Naval Auxiliary Program is actively addressing the problem.

How can sufficient shipboard containers be acquired rapidly in a contingency situation? The total U.S. container inventory is more than sufficient to handle military requirements in a war or mobilization, and it is also adequate should a nonmobilization contingency occur. But quick availability is the problem. A partial solution has been to require shipping firms that commit containerships under the Sealift Readiness Program also to commit three times the number of containers that each committed ship can carry, and two-thirds as many chassis as containers. Even so, there can be no guarantee that a shipping firm's containers, which are typically dispersed worldwide, can be marshalled quickly. Should the number of container shipping firms participating in the program decline, the problem would become more acute.

---

[8] A key consideration in solving this problem is how to obtain and position the number of lighters required to offload RO/RO vessels and containerships where there are no deepwater piers. Lighters such as the landing craft utility (LCU) can do the job but have little peacetime use. Funds to build and maintain them may be difficult to justify.

[9] National Research Council, *Containership Underway Replenishment: A Study of the Use of Containerships for the Underway Replenishment of Naval Vessels* (Washington, D.C.: National Academy of Sciences, 1971).

Land System Problems. Transportation components in the intermodal land system are the railroad and highway carrier. DOD's in-house transport capability in the continental United States, when compared with the private sector, is small. DOD does operate an interchange rail fleet and own a small number of containers and chassis, but requirements in a contingency would far exceed this limited inventory. As in the past, continental U.S. transport requirements will fall primarily upon the private sector. Problems include the following:

In peacetime, will a sufficient number of commercial containers be available to handle normal DOD requirements? The 1973–74 container shortfall has already been described. And while the combination of circumstances that brought about this shortage was unique, the possibility of a future shortfall cannot be ruled out. The very possibility of a shortfall makes planning on the use of containers in a contingency a high-risk alternative.

How can the container distribution system be adapted for the movement of military cargo that will not fit into a standard size (eight by eight) closed dry van container? This type accounts for approximately 95 percent of the U.S. container inventory. A partial solution was to use the flat rack or platform container. The 1972 *Sealift Procurement and National Security (SPANS)* study estimated that using flat racks or platform containers for the movement of wheeled, tracked, and other types of military outsize cargo could shorten the deployment time of American forces significantly. Considerably more military cargo could move on containerships if flat racks were available. In 1974, however, there were only 4,063 flat racks in the U.S. container inventory, or 1.06 percent of the total. In 1976, an optimistic estimate would put the figure at no more than 5,000.[10] The commercial sector does not require a large inventory of this type of container for peacetime use. The 1972 *SPANS* study recommended that DOD acquire 15,000 flat racks at an estimated cost of $50 million,[11] and later DOD studies have made the same recommendation.

How can commercial containers be used in the movement of ammunition? Most of the 6,700 MILVANS owned by DOD are certified to carry ammunition, and another 20,000 civilian-owned containers could probably be used. This inventory, however, falls far short of the number that would be needed in a war or prolonged con-

---

[10] U.S. Department of Commerce, Maritime Administration, *Inventory of American Intermodal Equipment 1975* (Washington, D.C.: U.S. Government Printing Office, 1975), p. 40.

[11] U.S. Department of Defense, *Sealift Procurement and National Security (SPANS)*, Part III, "Defense Implications," p. I–38.

tingency. Containerizing ammunition shipments is probably cost-effective. In 1975, some 160 MILVANS of ammunition were shipped to Europe every forty-five days. Savings in this pilot program and improvements in efficiency were encouraging.[12] The long-run problem, however, is how to adapt a commercial container quickly and economically to the stringent requirements of the Coast Guard and the American Association of Railroads for movement of ammunition. The DOD project manager for developing a surface container distribution system undertook in 1974–75 to develop an efficient and economical ammunition-restraint system with commercial containers.

How can DOD containerized cargo be monitored? Maintaining current information on the location of containerized cargo, particularly cargo in transit, is a problem not only for DOD but also for the commercial sector. Most commercial firms use an optical scanner that reads coded marks or labels on the outside of the container or vehicle as it passes. Information such as serial number and content can be recorded and transmitted to management. This system was relatively inexpensive and about 90 percent accurate. The scanner, however, must be precisely located in relation to the moving container or vehicle. It cannot pick up markings, for example, within twenty feet on either side of its line of sight. Another problem is dirt accumulation on labels, which can cause erroneous readings. The Army Mobility Equipment Research and Development Center at Fort Belvoir, Va., has been at work on a portable scanner using microwave transmissions to identify container labels. It would have a capability of scanning within a range, simultaneously reading the labels on the cargo container and the vehicle.[13] Weather effects like dirt and snow would not impair the accuracy of the system.

How can containers transporting military cargo be kept moving in the system? As a general rule, much more DOD cargo is shipped from the continental United States to overseas destinations than is shipped back. In peacetime, this imbalance can be partially corrected by using the same containers that moved DOD cargo overseas to return commercial cargo to the United States. Pre-positioning containers worldwide to take care of anticipated demands is a continuing problem for commercial carriers and would arise to some extent whether military cargo were in the system or not. In wartime, however, the problem of returning containers to the continental United States from

---

12 Morris, "Containers," *Defense Transportation Journal*, p. 14.

13 "Portable Scanner 'Sees' Shipments," *Army Logistician*, vol. 9 (May–June 1975), p. 39.

overseas theaters of operation would become critical.[14] A container shortage could slow down or even halt shipments overseas. Another problem would be congestion at loading points where empty return containers compete for dock space with loaded containers. If the system were functioning with minimal or no delays, that is, if containers on arriving land carriers were promptly unloaded and replaced by empty containers and moved out of the port area, then serious problems probably would not occur. If, however, significant delays were introduced into the system, for whatever reason, ports could become blocked, as was the case with some ports on the East Coast in World War I and some ports in Vietnam.

Air System Problems. The intermodal air system, in its infancy, probably would not play a significant part in a contingency or mobilization before 1980.[15] The major impediment to expanding this system is that no airplane in the U.S. (or world) inventory is designed to carry containers. There are, however, airplanes such as the 747F and the proposed DC-10-30AF that can accept containers.[16] No present or proposed commercial airplane can accept the roll on/roll off highway van trailer.

To establish a framework for planning an air intermodal system, the Department of Transportation, in cooperation with the air force, sponsored Project INTACT (Intermodal Air Cargo Test) in 1973. The air force C-5A, which can accept highway trailers, was used in a commercial test to make five determinations: the acceptability of air shipment of intermodal containers, the physical characteristics of such containers, the necessary economical parameters of such a system, the requirement for ground handling of the containers, and the design parameters of the optimum commercial air freighter of the future that could double in a national emergency as a Civil Reserve Air Fleet cargo transport.[17]

Loading and unloading both roll on/roll off and marine-type containers were successfully demonstrated in April and May 1975, and a

---

[14] For an Atlantic or Mediterranean contingency, containerships might load on the East Coast, return to Gulf or South Atlantic ports, and then load and return to East Coast ports.

[15] Military cargo moved by air should not be confused with military cargo moved *in containers* by air. The 1973 Israeli airlift conclusively demonstrated that military cargo, particularly outsize cargo, can be effectively air transported. This capability is a key element in DOD mobilization and contingency planning.

[16] Seaboard World Airlines and Lufthansa were operating a land-air-land intermodal system in 1975.

[17] U.S. Department of Transportation, *Project INTACT Loading Demonstration*, Dover AFB, Delaware, April 16, 1975, p. 1.

flight demonstration was successfully completed in October 1975. The air force had responsibility for developing the land-air-land intermodal system for the military.

Summary. By and large the most important problems involve use of containers in a contingency or in wartime. There are, however, other problems, in achieving an economical as well as a viable system:

Can some military equipment marginally too large for containerization be redesigned to fit into a container?

Is it cost-effective to use the container as a portable warehouse, in particular, a leased commercial container? If it is not cost-effective to use commercial containers, does this imply a need for an increase in DOD's container inventory? Is the relatively expensive MILVAN the best option open?

Can savings be achieved by developing container modules that, when put together, equal the standard eight-by-eight-by-twenty (or forty) container dimensions? The army is experimenting with the so-called TRICON, a 40-foot container in three sections.

Can container-system support equipment be standardized among the modes and between DOD and the commercial sector? Examples would include lifters and side loaders that perform such chores as stacking containers in storage areas and loading a container aboard an aircraft. Note also that the solution to the over-the-shore discharge of containerships problem will require development and testing of a considerable amount of hardware. Before new military equipment is developed, commercial equipment should be examined for adaptability to military requirements.

Maximizing DOD use of containers for its transport needs will require solutions to some very large problems and to many smaller ones as well.

Developing a DOD Container Distribution System

It is established policy that DOD cargo will be containerized for transportation whenever possible because movement of cargo in containers is cost-effective in peacetime. Relying on containers for cargo movement in a war or contingency, however, introduces an element of risk which must be removed or reduced to manageable proportions. The DOD container distribution system should be capable of interfacing with the commercial system, meeting DOD peacetime requirements, and supporting DOD contingency or wartime requirements. In particular, it should be capable of a quick response.

In the early years of the so-called container revolution, each service addressed these problems independently, as in development of the CONEX and MILVAN by the army. In 1973 the newly established DOD project manager for developing a surface container distribution system was directed to find solutions to a number of container-related problems. The project group was staffed by personnel drawn from all of the services. In 1974, however, responsibility for some problem areas was transferred to other agencies within DOD and the charter of the project manager was terminated on July 1, 1975. Since then, all container systems problems have been tasked to the services or the transportation operating agencies. The navy has the responsibility for finding a solution to the offshore discharge of containerships problem; the army, for developing a container ammunition distribution system; and the air force, as originally, for developing the land-air-land system. The Military Traffic Management Command has responsibility for developing the interface with rail and highway systems in the continental United States, acquisition of commercial facilities in a contingency, and documentation of container movements. The Military Sealift Command is the interface between DOD and the commercial containership fleet owner.[18]

There is no unanimous agreement within DOD on which management approach—project manager or tasking individual services and agencies—is preferable, though the present fragmented approach is contrary to past policy when the problem addressed was DOD-wide and cut across service lines.

---

[18] Morris, "Containers," *Defense Transportation Journal*, p. 18. The chain of command runs from the service to a four-man joint container-coordination group, to a joint container steering group, then to a logistics systems policy committee, which interfaces with the assistant secretary of defense for installations and logistics.

8
SHIPYARDS

Although naval shipyards are not considered part of the defense transportation system, their operation is relevant in an examination of duplication between government and private transportation sectors.

The first naval shipyard was established at Portsmouth, N.H., in 1800. Private shipbuilding in the U.S., however, antedates this effort by more than 100 years. Colonial shipbuilders supplied tonnage not only for their own ventures but also for English shipowners. There were 600,000 gross tons of English shipping in 1770, and approximately 210,000 tons were constructed in North America.[1] Since the nation's independence, naval and private shipyards have developed side by side.

Support for the private yards was tied very early to support for the merchant marine. In 1817, the Congress prohibited vessels not documented and built in the United States to engage in American coastal or intercoastal trade. This prohibition was later extended to Hawaii, Alaska, and the islands of the Caribbean. Section 27 of the Merchant Marine Act of 1920 reaffirmed the intent of Congress in this respect. The Merchant Marine Act of 1936 asserted the necessity for a U.S. shipbuilding industry and required that vessels receiving an operating differential subsidy under the act be "built American." And the Merchant Marine Act of 1970 directed the secretary of commerce to develop a shipbuilding program that will support the "creation and maintenance of efficient shipbuilding and repair capacity in the United States with adequate numbers of skilled personnel to provide an adequate mobilization base."[2]

In its early years, U.S. shipbuilding was competitive on world

---

[1] McDowell and Gibbs, *Ocean Transportation*, p. 21.

[2] *Merchant Marine Act of 1970*, Section 210.

markets. The American-built clipper of the 1850s was one of the most sought-after ships ever constructed. The decline of the merchant marine after the Civil War, however, also signalled the decline of American shipbuilding. The construction of competitively priced steel and steam merchant ships passed to the British and European yards. The extent of American noncompetitiveness was indicated in the Merchant Marine Act of 1936, which allowed payment by the government of a construction-differential subsidy of up to 50 percent. In some cases, ships built in American yards cost twice as much as similar ships built overseas. The Merchant Marine Act of 1970 established a Shipbuilding Commission to review the status of American shipyards and their progress toward increasing productivity. The commission was to determine whether the industry could improve productivity enough to reduce the maximum construction differential to 35 percent by FY 1976.[3]

Naval shipyards employ civilian labor under civil service contract, and yard operations are directed by a small contingent of naval personnel, mostly line and engineering officers. The primary mission of the naval shipyard is to support the fleet both in peacetime and in times of emergency. It can build, repair, alter, or convert naval vessels as the need arises. The yard is a completely integrated industrial plant, with a full range of shop, engineering, and design facilities. Although all yards have a broad fleet-support capability, each yard has tended to specialize over the years. The naval shipyard at Portsmouth, N.H., for example, is used principally for overhaul and conversion of submarines.

In the twentieth century, the concept of the naval shipyard as a purely industrial operation has been expanded to include supply and provisioning of ships and providing medical and dental services to shipboard personnel. In World War II, the role of the yards was further enlarged in terms of additional service and administrative facilities. Today, several yards have, in effect, become naval operating bases offering all services necessary to support the fleet.

Historically, the Congress has supported the concept of naval shipyards, not indirectly as in the case of the private sector, but by granting the necessary appropriations to maintain the yards consistent with their defined missions. Only after World War II did the cost of work performed in the naval yards, that is, the economic efficiency of the yards, become a major issue.

---

[3] *Merchant Marine Act of 1970*, Section 41. In 1974 it was predicted that some high-technology vessels such as liquid natural gas carriers might ultimately be constructed in U.S. yards without subsidy.

The Industry Today

Congress has found both naval and private shipyards to be in the national interest. During a war or emergency, private yards are vital to fleet support, as well as being responsible for building and maintaining a merchant marine. Private yards, together with their naval counterparts, are the nation's shipbuilding and ship-repair mobilization base. How best to maintain this mobilization base in peacetime, particularly in a time of tight defense budgets, has become a difficult question.

Beginning in the mid-1960s, a number of steps were taken to maintain private shipyards while preserving the naval shipyard. In 1964, Congress mandated that at least 35 percent of ship conversion, alteration, and repair money should be spent in private yards. Although the requirement was repealed in 1967, the Department of Defense issued instructions in the same year that at least 30 percent of this type of work was to be allocated to the private sector. In 1974, Congress formally set 30 percent as a minimum, and, since 1968, all new naval construction has been assigned to commercial yards.

The assignment of a portion of naval repair and conversion work and all new construction to the private yards, together with the decrease in the fleet to the smallest size since before Pearl Harbor, had predictable consequences. Naval shipyards at Boston, Mass.; Brooklyn, N.Y.; and Hunters Point, Calif., were closed. Table 5 indicates the status of naval and private shipyards in 1974 in numbers, employment, and division of naval work.

Who Shall Build, Repair, Alter, and Convert?

In hearings before the Seapower Subcommittee of the House Committee on Armed Services in the summer of 1974, the question of who shall build, repair, alter, and convert naval vessels again arose. The central issue was a proposal by the private shipyards that the Congress mandate at least 50 percent of naval repair and alteration work to the private sector. The response of proponents of naval shipyards was predictable. Representative Robert L. Leggett (Democrat, California) bluntly stated his reaction to the proposed fifty-fifty split:

> Mr. Chairman, unfortunately there is still a competition between Navy and private shipyards. The advent of 65/35 on repairs, alterations, and conversions led to the closing of Brooklyn and San Diego in the middle 1960s. Portsmouth was scheduled also. Two years ago an effort was pioneered

Table 5

NAVAL AND PRIVATE SHIPYARDS, 1974

	Naval	Private
Number of yards	8 [a]	192 [b]
Employment	59,799	148,900 [c]
New construction work (dollar value in percent)	0	100
Conversion, repair, and alteration (dollar value in percent)	68.3	31.7

[a] Portsmouth, N.H.; Philadelphia, Pa.; Norfolk, Va.; Charleston, S.C.; Long Beach, Calif.; Mare Island, Calif.; Puget Sound, Wash.; Pearl Harbor, Hawaii.

[b] There were nineteen major yards capable of building ships 400 feet or longer, of which six held contracts for new navy construction.

[c] Major yards employ 105,000 of the 148,900 total employees.

Source: U.S. Congress, House, Seapower Subcommittee of Committee on Armed Services, *Hearings, Current Status of Shipyards 1974,* 3 Parts, 93d Cong., 2d sess., July, August, September 1974, Part 1, p. 11; Part 2, pp. 631, 647.

at 50-50 even though the big private yards had been hogging 100 percent of the new ship construction since 1967.

The effort failed last year, but as I understand the same tune is being played to this committee in spite of the fact that the private share of repairs and alterations at 29.98 percent was the largest share ever received by them. Dollarwise, the privates received in this one category almost 100 percent more than they had received for the 6-year average immediately preceding.

It is frankly comical and puzzling to many of us in this room how any serious consideration can be given to this new, outrageous, gouging demand by *private enterprise* [italics supplied].[4]

The value of the work in question for FY 1975 was $1.23 billion. Navy yards were programmed to receive about $860 million and the private sector about $368 million. An annual repair and alteration budget of over $1 billion is difficult to apportion. A move one way or the other could cause the closing of one or more naval or private yards, if the total shipyard work remained constant. Employment of thousands of skilled workers would be affected, and many would leave the industry rather than move to new locations. In either case,

---

[4] U.S. Congress, House, Subcommittee of the Committee on Appropriations, *Hearings on Department of Defense Appropriations for 1975,* 93d Cong., 2d sess., May 1974, p. 280.

the U.S. shipyard mobilization base would be decreased, both in yards and in the pool of skilled manpower needed in a mobilization. And finally, casting a very long shadow over the entire question was the rapid buildup of Soviet naval strength, not only in vessels at sea but also in fleet-support facilities ashore. In 1974, the Soviet Union had 16 major shipyards and 200 smaller ones, employing approximately 215,000 skilled workers. The navy considered these facilities equal to any in the world.[5]

The issue of what will be the proper mix in the U.S. shipbuilding base between naval and private yards is still an open question. The wide-ranging and sometimes illuminating hearings of 1974 produced no final answers.

The Case for Private Yards

The case for shifting more naval work to the private sector rests on two arguments. First, the cost of work in naval yards ranges between 20 and 100 percent more than in private yards. Second, without additional work many private shipyards will be forced to close, thus reducing the nation's mobilization base.

In asserting that private yards are more cost-effective than naval yards, the Shipbuilder's Council of America relies on four studies by independent public accounting and management consulting firms between 1962 and 1972. The studies agreed that work in naval yards was more costly, but disagreed over how much more. One study did not break down its data into categories of new construction, conversion, or repairs. Overall, it found that naval yards were 20 to 28 percent more costly. Another study determined that new construction in naval shipyards cost approximately 35.7 percent more than in private yards. Still another study found significant differences between private and naval yards in the cost of a production worker hour and man hours expended on similar jobs, concluding that naval shipyard cumulative costs could be 109 to 124 percent higher than costs in private yards. A 1972 study estimated the conversion differential to be between 15 and 115 percent; the repair differential, 23 percent; and the new construction differential, 40 percent.[6] But, after 1968, all

---

[5] U.S. Congress, House, Seapower Subcommittee of Committee on Armed Services, *Hearings on Current Status of Shipyards 1974, Part 1,* 93d Cong., 2d sess., July 1974, pp. 145–47. For another comparison of U.S. and Soviet shipyard capabilities, see Norman Polmar, *Soviet Naval Power: Challenge for the 1970s* (New York: Crane, Russak & Co., 1973), p. 125.

[6] House, Seapower Subcommittee of Committee on Armed Services, *Hearings on Shipyards, Part 2,* p. 646. The firms were Ernst and Ernst, Arthur Andersen, and Booz-Allen.

new navy construction was let to the private sector, and the question of higher naval costs for new construction became moot.

Of the seventeen major private yards operating in 1975, fourteen were divisions of large multiproduct corporations, such as Lockheed, General Dynamics, and Litton Industries. In the short run at least, funds from the parent firm could cushion the effect of decreased revenues from naval work. The varying impact of naval work on small and large yards was noted by Edwin Hood, president of the Shipbuilders' Council. He emphasized that the smaller private yards had the largest stake in how the navy's nonconstruction dollar was allocated:

> It is important to state, and perhaps emphasize that most of the yards whose principal livelihoods depend on this type of work, both naval and merchant, are not those that build ships. Some 192 companies have a master ship repair certification from the Navy, and it is this group of shipyards which have continuously challenged, and properly so in the view of our board of directors, the disproportionate distribution of work favoring higher cost naval shipyards.[7]

An adequate shipyard mobilization base is a straightforward matter in the view of the private yards, particularly the smaller ones: unless more work is forthcoming, many will have to shut down. In testimony before the House Subcommittee on Appropriations, when it was considering the FY 1975 defense budget, representatives of ship-repair yards in the New England, New York, and New Jersey area all stressed their needs for additional work. The president of the New England Ship Repair Yard Association stated, "The New England ship repair yards are in a disaster area." Testimony by a representative of West Coast yards was in a similar vein. He called the 1973 congressionally mandated 30 percent of naval repair work to private yards "a lifesaver."

Michael J. Gallagher, president of the New York and New Jersey Drydock Association, testified:

> We bring before your committee the fact that if a national emergency existed today, the Government-operated naval shipyards could not properly support the defense of this Nation without the aid of private shipyards.
>
> A realistic allocation of funds from the proposed naval repair, overhaul, and alteration budget to the private shipyards is necessary to maintain this private industrial base as

---

[7] House, Seapower Subcommittee of Committee on Armed Services, *Hearings on Shipyards, Part 2*, p. 647.

has been demonstrated time and again. I ask this committee to act vigorously in effecting this allocation.[8]

While not necessarily agreeing with the estimates cited above, the navy did acknowledge that ship repair work and new construction cost more in naval yards. How important additional naval work is to the survival of private yards, particularly the smaller ones, is more difficult to determine. One fact weighing heavily on the question is the low profitability of the shipbuilding industry in general. Hood asserted that profit in the ship repair and ship construction industry is "one half of one percent . . . on sales after taxes."[9] A more detailed study published in 1975 came to the same conclusion. Using data from four shipyards, it indicated that in 1973 the profit on sales before taxes averaged 1.9 percent and concluded that "profits in the shipbuilding industry have been low since the 1960s, and the higher-risk government work has been less profitable than commercial work."[10]

If these low profitability margins continue and if private yard capacity continues to go unused, a number of yards may be expected to close.[11] On the other hand, navy yards, which are congressionally funded, need not make a profit sufficient to keep resources employed in their shipbuilding and repair industry. The question whether all 192 private yards are necessary as a mobilization base is another matter. Perhaps some marginal yards could close without appreciable effect.

The Case for Naval Shipyards

The role of the naval shipyard as defined by Rear Admiral Robert C. Gooding, commander, Naval Sea Systems Command, is "overhauling and repairing our complex combatant ships and installing, maintaining and checking our sophisticated electronics and missile weapons systems." He justified naval shipyards in these words:

Since the earliest years of the Federal Government, both executive and legislative branches recognized the need to

[8] House, Subcommittee of the Committee on Appropriations, *Hearings on Defense Appropriations for 1975*, p. 327.

[9] House, Seapower Subcommittee of Committee on Armed Services, *Hearings on Shipyards, Part 2*, p. 650.

[10] John J. Palmieri, "Commercial Shipbuilders; Risk and Reward," *U.S. Naval Institute Proceedings*, vol. 101 (August 1975), p. 55.

[11] Although the yards vary in size and other respects, and each has its own average cost curve, underutilization generally can be expected to raise average operating costs.

maintain Government-owned, Government-operated, and Government-funded shipyards to aid in the defense of the Nation. This policy has been consistently supported through the years by means of congressional appropriations. This support has permitted each naval shipyard to develop as an integrated plant with a full range of shop facilities and a full range of engineering, design, and shop personnel skills in keeping with its mission.[12]

Although the role of the privately owned shipyards is recognized as essential to fleet support in an emergency, the navy opposes any rigid limitation on the assignment of work as between naval and private yards. Arguments supporting retention of naval shipyards include the following:

(1) Naval shipyards are available for new construction and repairs when private yards are fully booked, as in the period 1973–74. Historically, in periods of high utilization of private yards, skilled labor shortages have developed, and navy work has been delayed. Such delays could adversely affect the fleet mission and general readiness if they involved an aircraft carrier or a nuclear-missile submarine.

(2) Many private yards, given a choice, prefer to build and repair commercial vessels, and the navy is thereby limited in its options in the private sector (this issue is explored in the following section, Navy Procurement Practices).

(3) Naval shipyards have a full range of crew support facilities, that is, facilities for berthing and messing of crews as well as medical and dental services.

(4) In an emergency, a naval yard will give priority to a naval vessel, but there is no guarantee that a private yard would.

(5) Naval shipyards promise better service for navy ships. The modern naval ship is technologically complex, and special skills are required to perform their overhaul and repair work. Although some private yards possess this capability, most do not. In many cases, the private yard that can handle, or will bid, on such repairs is geographically distant from naval shore-support facilities.

(6) Naval yards are less prone to work stoppages than are private yards.

(7) Naval yards provide a yardstick to measure the performance of private yards.

(8) Naval yards support the navy's homeport policy, indirectly helping to keep experienced personnel in the service. Ship repair and

---

[12] House, Seapower Subcommittee of Committee on Armed Services, *Hearings On Shipyards*, Part 1, p. 12.

overhaul work is scheduled typically at a naval yard in the ship's home port area, where crew families are usually domiciled.

Deputy Secretary of Defense William P. Clements, Jr., stated the general case for the naval shipyard: "The higher cost differentials for naval shipyards are, in effect, the insurance premium that the Government pays to have a strategically located shipyard with an assured capability of giving *immediate* [italics supplied] industrial support to naval ships."[13]

A part of the navy's case in 1974 for preserving naval shipyards rested on the argument that private yards had a backlog of work and that it was difficult to place navy work. This argument, however, presupposed that 1974 levels of work in private yards would continue indefinitely, and that has not been the case. Normally, the industry has excess capacity. In 1970, for example, it was estimated that less than 70 percent of shipyard capacity was being used, and capacity had decreased markedly from its 1945 high. Moreover, the demand for shipyard services is cyclical, tending to follow the demand for ocean shipping, which itself depends largely on world economic conditions. The 1973–74 recession reduced demand for ocean shipping and the attendant demand for shipyard services. Large numbers of construction orders were cancelled worldwide. At least one major American shipyard required federal assistance to remain solvent.

As to the argument that private yards are reluctant to bid on or accept navy work, between 65 and 75 percent of private yard work in the period 1964–70 was for the navy. If there is a reluctance, the relevant question is Why? Why did the proportion of navy work in private yards drop to about 45 percent in 1975? Another argument asserts a shortage of skilled workers in private yards, a shortage which contributes to rescheduling and work delays. But this condition in 1974 could hardly be considered permanent. Data simply do not support the thesis of chronic labor shortages in the shipbuilding and repair industry. Moreover, it cannot be persuasively argued that employees of private yards cannot acquire the necessary skills to repair and overhaul the modern naval vessel, or that naval shipyards in general have unique capabilities. The testimony of John V. Banks, president of National Steel and Shipbuilding Company, is instructive in this respect:

> In 1965, the naval repair facility at San Diego, located adjacent to our shipyard, was closed. The unique facility possessed by the Navy in this repair facility was a graving dock

---

[13] House, Subcommittee of the Committee on Appropriations, *Hearings on Defense Appropriations for 1975*, p. 298.

and there was no other located in the San Diego area. After extensive efforts, the graving dock was leased by the Navy to the San Diego Port District which operates it on a toll basis for use by private shipyards in the area which are engaged in Navy repair work on a competitive basis. During the years since the repair facility at San Diego was closed, the size of the fleet home ported in San Diego has been substantially increased and the fleet has participated in the Vietnam War, with a substantial repair requirement during these hostilities. I know of no substantial complaint on the part of the Navy as to the adequacy of repair support by the private shipyards in the San Diego area.[14]

The strongest argument in support of naval shipyards is that an operating fleet requires priority consideration under any and all circumstances. Having some capability of its own is particularly important in peacetime, when it has no authority to commandeer private facilities. This is not to suggest that a private yard would turn away a major combatant vessel in an emergency situation. In less clear-cut cases, however, disputes could arise about the need for, and the degrees of, priority, and honest men could reasonably disagree. Deputy Secretary of Defense Clements summed it up well when he said that the naval shipyard is an insurance policy against the unforeseen. He did not indicate, however, how many naval shipyards it would take to provide the insurance.

Navy Procurement Practices

How the navy procures services from the private shipyard industry would not normally be discussed in a debate on the merits of maintaining a naval ship repair capability. It is relevant, however, because one of the navy's chief arguments for maintaining its own yards is that private yards, given an option, prefer to work for the Maritime Administration and to build and repair for private accounts. Keeping an in-house capability for the navy, then, would seem necessary. But why should private industry be reluctant to do naval work?

Many private shipyards, in particular the smaller repair yards, actively seek navy work. Although they might have serious grievances about how the navy procures and administers its contracts, they would not turn down work if it were available. The chief source of reluctance is from the larger yards, which have the capability to build tech-

---

[14] House, Seapower Subcommittee of Committee on Armed Services, *Hearings on Shipyards*, Part 2, p. 707.

nologically complex modern naval vessels. These are the yards that prefer non-navy work.

Private shipyards are profit-oriented ventures. Like any other business enterprise they must in the long run earn a return on capital invested. Other things being equal, shipyard management is indifferent, in fact must be indifferent, whether it builds and repairs for the navy, the Maritime Administration, or private interests. The point, however, is that other things are not equal. Many yards doing business with the navy claim they not only did not earn profits but in fact incurred losses.

Executive officers of the nation's large private shipyards, one after the other, testified before the Seapower Subcommittee against navy procurement methods. The testimony of John P. Diesel, president of Newport News Shipbuilding and Drydock Company, was typical.

> Unrealistic target prices are responsible in large part for the dire situation now facing the Navy's shipbuilding program. Having chronically underestimated shipbuilding costs over the past 5 to 10 years, the Navy has not requested from Congress and thus never received adequate funds to pay the full costs of these new ships. The shipbuilders and their suppliers have been left holding the bill. Now that bill is being presented to the Navy in the form of claims totaling well in excess of $1 billion for formal and constructive changes, equitable adjustments and the like.
>
> In the last 10 years the Navy and other Government agencies have moved unceasingly toward total direction and control of the shipbuilder—or "engagement" as the Navy terms this intrusion. Administrative redundancy, confusion, fragmentation of authority, frustration, and an ever-growing mountain of reports and memorandums—and in the final analysis increased cost—has been the result.
>
> The Navy has attempted to impose on us management control systems, developed in other industries, which serve no useful purpose and are very expensive. Indeed, it is conceivable that the cost of complying with all these management systems and the related paperwork required for a major combatant ship could approach the cost of the ship itself.
>
> We find particularly frustrating the fact that while the Navy effectively exercised direction and control of many day to day decisions, it often refused to accept the responsibility for those decisions.
>
> We are very concerned that the actual or implied exercise of this power by the Government has given rise to a subtle

form of intimidation to achieve compliance with its desires in contract matters.

After making these general criticisms, Diesel attacked several specific navy practices.

> Navy supervision and direction have become particularly burdensome with respect to our purchasing and subcontracting activities. Newport News Shipbuilding processes 36,000 purchase orders a year to approximately 6,000 vendors in virtually every State. Roughly 40 percent of our total cost is paid to our vendors.
>
> Perhaps no area of ship construction and procurement holds out more opportunity for reduction of costs and delays than change orders. . . . The sheer number and scope of formal contract change orders is a continuing problem. There have now been more than 1,200 Government-recognized changes on the *Nimitz* and roughly 2,400 on the DLGN 36 class. We estimate the *Nimitz* changes—some of which have required major rearrangements of the ship—have affected more than 15,000 drawings.
>
> The Navy has utilized ground rules and standards of proof which make equitable resolution of these matters terribly time consuming. Settlement has sometimes been delayed for years. In 1972 we finally resolved a claim in excess of $7 million relative to the aircraft carrier *Ranger* which had been pending since 1958—almost 14 years since it had been submitted to the Navy. . . . We are in effect financing Navy work to the extent of $115 million at an effective interest rate of 14 percent as a result of the Navy's inaction in this matter. . . .

In conclusion, Diesel stated: "Either the Navy—hopefully prompted by Congress—will develop fair, straightforward and even-handed ship procurement policies or it will eventually build all its own ships and the principal components as well."[15]

As the shipyard shortage tightened in 1974, the charge was raised that DOD, in an attempt to secure private yard bids on naval work, was withholding steel priorities for merchant ship construction. Construction of three Liquid Natural Gas Carriers (LNG) by the Newport

---

[15] House, Seapower Subcommittee of Committee on Armed Services, *Hearings on Shipyards, Part 2*, pp. 925–938. For a recent review of the causes of shipbuilders' claims against the navy, see Comptroller General of the United States, *Status of Shipbuilders' Claims For Price Increases: Settlement Progress, Navy Claim Prevention Actions, Need For Caution* (Washington, D.C.: U.S. General Accounting Office, 1975). In April 1976, there were three major unsettled shipbuilders' claims totaling $1.8 billion. DOD has requested approximately $1 billion from Congress to settle the claims.

News shipyard was said to have been delayed for this reason.[16] Testifying before the Seapower Subcommittee in October 1974, Admiral Hyman Rickover responded to this charge and the earlier criticism of naval procurement practices by the shipbuilding industry. The navy would not recommend assigning a priority to future large tankers or LNGs, he said, because such ships have no national defense purpose. As for LNGs already under construction, he said, an agreement was worked out with Newport News Shipbuilding whereby the yard "would not allow performance of work on non-Navy contracts to interfere with the performance of work necessary to meet Newport News commitments on Navy contracts."[17]

With respect to charges leveled by the industry, Admiral Rickover declared:

> As for the Navy work, some shipbuilders may be experiencing losses or in any event less profit than they originally anticipated. These problems they attribute to inflation, inappropriate defense procurement policies, improper administration of shipbuilding contracts by the Navy, and a host of other reasons, all of which they contend are beyond the shipbuilders' control. As shipbuilders present the case, the blame falls squarely on the Navy, not the shipbuilders.
>
> Faced with this situation, shipbuilders want the Government to guarantee that they will, under no circumstances, incur any losses.
>
> This can be done by changing all of their contracts, as they have suggested, into cost-plus contracts—or by either using the claims route, or obtaining extracontractual relief under Public Law 85-804.
>
> Some shipbuilders appear to be trying to attain their desired ends in a less obtrusive manner—through omnibus claims. In preparing such claims, shipbuilders dredge up everything they can to blame contract losses on the Navy.

Responding to criticisms of navy change orders, Admiral Rickover said:

> From the shipbuilder's standpoint, the best basis for large claims is to tie them to Navy change orders. Because of the length of time for ship construction and because of the continual updating of ship specifications to meet changing defense needs, changes are and always will be an inherent part of ship construction.

---

[16] For a summary of this allegation, see "The Supertanker Steel Squeeze," *Business Week*, May 18, 1974, pp. 28–29.

[17] House, Seapower Subcommittee of Committee on Armed Services, *Hearings on Shipyards, Part 3*, p. 1286.

However, even if it were possible to build warships without changes, I suspect that the shipbuilders would not really like to delete the changes clause since that would remove a major vehicle which they use to develop omnibus, after the fact claims to try to recover overruns.

Admiral Rickover concluded with a comment on Newport News Shipbuilding:

> The basic reasons Newport News is having financial problems on their new construction contracts are that, (1) the productivity has decreased substantially during their large manpower buildup, (2) Newport News did not achieve the buildup of skilled manpower they needed to build their ships according to the contract schedules, and (3) the overhead increased from about 56 percent when Tenneco bought Newport News in 1968 to the current overhead of about 86 percent. These are contractor-responsible items, not the fault of the Navy.[18]

Admiral James L. Holloway, chief of naval operations, was more conciliatory toward the private yards.

> Nevertheless, it is apparent from the attitude of the industry toward Navy work that there must be a degree of validity to their position. Taken individually, each of the many governmental administrative requirements levied on the contractors is well conceived and motivated. Each is aimed at delivery of a quality product, in a reasonable time, at a reasonable cost, while protecting Government interests. However, in the aggregate, they may very well constitute an unnecessarily expensive and perhaps a counterproductive burden on the shipbuilders.[19]

It is not the purpose here to sort out conflicting testimony about DOD procurement practices. The interested reader is referred to the extensive 1971 and 1974 Seapower Subcommittee hearings on the status of American shipyards.[20] Even here much information necessary to an informed judgment is lacking. One point, however, is not in

---

[18] House, Seapower Subcommittee of Committee on Armed Services, *Hearings on Shipyards, Part 3*, pp. 1262–1267.

[19] House, Seapower Subcommittee of Committee on Armed Services, *Hearings on Shipyards, Part 3*, p. 1519.

[20] Two brief summaries of the dispute over procurement practices between the navy and the shipbuilding industry can be found in "Civilian Shipbuilders Mutiny Against Navy," *U.S. News and World Report*, September 9, 1974, pp. 51–52, and "The Shipyard Gap and How It Grew," *Seapower*, August 8, 1974, pp. 28–33.

dispute. Writing in the August 1975 issue of the *U.S. Naval Institute Proceedings*, Captain John J. Palmieri, USN, made this observation:

> When a shipbuilder negotiates with a private shipowner, they negotiate as equals. All matters of importance in their contractual relationship are subject to negotiation, including the type of contract, ship design, delivery schedule, and price. However, when the government contracts for ships, it does so not as an equal but as a sovereign—one entitled to independent authority. While this is a valid concept where matters of national interest are paramount, it is sometimes used in contractual matters where the basis of mutuality should apply.[21]

The chief of naval operations has named five strategic and operational requirements with respect to shipyards: two shipyards on each coast capable of repairing aircraft carriers; one shipyard on each coast capable of repairing surface nuclear ships; three shipyards on each coast capable of overhauling nuclear submarines; three shipyards on each coast capable of installing, maintaining, and checking out sophisticated electronics and missile weapons systems; and shipyards to serve major homeport and operating areas.[22]

The eight naval shipyards operating in 1976, together with major private yards, met this requirement. There remain these questions: (1) Could the requirements be met entirely by private yards? (2) Can the requirements be met at less cost, that is, can the present naval–private yard mixture become more efficient? (3) Is there justification on noneconomic grounds for maintaining some naval yard capability at higher cost? Or, to paraphrase Secretary Clements, can the premium paid on this type of insurance policy be defended?

Given time, private yards could meet all of the requirements, but at present they probably do not. However, does the shipbuilding and repair industry want to do away entirely with the navy's capability? This question was put to witnesses testifying on behalf of private yards. The response of Edwin Hood, president of the Shipbuilders Council, was typical. He categorically stated that the industry did not want to close all naval shipyards, adding: "If a capability in both sectors is to be appropriately preserved as a mobilization base, both must be appropriately sustained. A split of 70 to 85 percent of conversion, altera-

---

[21] Palmieri, "Commercial Shipbuilders," p. 50.

[22] House, Seapower Subcommittee of Committee on Armed Services, *Hearings on Shipyards, Part 1*, p. 587.

tion, and repair (CAR) work favoring 8 naval shipyards will never preserve 192 privately owned, commercially operated facilities."[23]

CAR work appears insufficient for optimal use of all naval and private yards, and navy officials cited underutilization of naval yards as one reason why their costs were higher. The same could be said of private yards. Overcapacity undoubtedly requires many yards to operate at higher than average cost, but other factors also contribute. Among them are yard management practices, both naval and private, together with naval procurement policies and the typical peaks and valleys of demand for repair and alteration work.

In his appearance before a House subcommittee on appropriations in May 1974, Admiral Rickover criticized private shipyard management, asserting that deficiencies exist "in nearly all aspects of shipyard operations." As for navy yard operations, the General Accounting Office, in an industrial management review of the Puget Sound Naval Shipyard, concluded that a number of steps could be taken to improve efficiency.[24] And in a little noted but instructive comment on naval and private shipyard management, an excellent case was made that "civilian, not naval officers should supervise ship overhauls." It concluded:

> The average naval shipyard ship superintendent seems to be a lieutenant/lieutenant commander who is getting his "ticket punched" for career development. He has fewer than three years experience, unless he has been slow to learn the ropes. Thus only the relatively inexperienced or inept are directly in charge of this most important period of a ship's life. Below him he has a myriad of civilian assistants, committees, branches, and divisions who, in effect, provide the specialized experience he lacks and further disperse his already limited authority. . . . This system, despite the often Herculean efforts of the ship superintendents trapped within it, generally produces as much paper as progress and subjects even the slightest change to the scrutiny and time consuming review of all but the gate guards.
>
> The current situation can be improved upon by doing away with the practice of assigning naval officers as ship superintendents. They would be replaced by a cadre of highly experienced, highly rated, and highly paid civilians

---

[23] House, Seapower Subcommittee of Committee on Armed Services, *Hearings on Shipyards, Part 2,* p. 648.

[24] Comptroller General of the United States, *Industrial Management Review of the Puget Sound Naval Shipyard* (Washington, D.C.: U.S. General Accounting Office, 1974), p. ii.

("master shipwrights") whose position would be an end in itself rather than a means to an end.[25]

The navy is moving to correct some of the more glaring inefficiencies of naval procurement policies, though the possibilities for improvement still seem boundless. Recall John Diesel remarked that the cost of meeting navy procurement and paper work requirements on a major combatant vessel might conceivably exceed the cost of the ship itself. If he is only 1 percent right, the realized savings would be significant.

Whether shipyard workload can be made more predictable is an open question. In recognition of the problem, the navy has developed several long-range plans for scheduling fleet overhaul and repair work. But as GAO found in its study of the Puget Sound yard, the problem is still to be resolved: "Since the most critical constraint on shipyard operations appears to be the level and predictability of workload, the greatest opportunities for improving overall shipyard productivity require stabilizing and increasing the workload, and developing a viable means of balancing manpower requirements with the workload."[26] Thus, evidence suggests that the chief of naval operations' strategic and operational requirements for U.S. shipyards can be met at less cost.

The last question was whether some naval shipyard capability can be justified on noneconomic grounds.

The strongest argument for maintaining naval yards is that these yards provide a fall-back repair and overhaul option. Should no such naval capability exist, the only alternative would be to enact standby legislation, which would allow the federal government to take over private facilities in less than mobilization situations. But, if an argument can be made for maintaining a naval repair capability, it probably can also be made for maintaining a limited naval construction capability. This brings the argument full circle and raises the basic issue, How much naval shipyard capability does the United States need? No witness appearing before the Seapower Subcommittee answered this question, nor will it be answered here, since quantifying such a capability would be a major task. An approach to the question, however, can be suggested: naval shipyards should be viewed primarily as a backstop to the nation's private yards, not as a major

---

[25] John L. MacMichael, "Civilians, Not Naval Officers Should Supervise Ship Overhauls," *U.S. Naval Institute Proceedings*, vol. 100 (October 1974), p. 83.

[26] Comptroller General of the U.S., *Industrial Management Review*, p. 33.

component in the mobilization base.[27] In this context, naval shipyard capability should be precisely defined, and, once defined, it should be utilized optimally, that is, sufficient work should be allocated to naval yards to insure operation at maximum efficiency.

Conclusion

If the mission of the naval shipyard is to augment the nation's private shipyards, and not to compete with them, then more naval yards will probably be closed. On the other hand, a limited shipbuilding capability might be restored to one or two of the remaining yards. This would shift more navy repair and overhaul work to the sector of the private shipbuilding industry that needs it most and would decrease navy reliance on the private sector for new construction. While this would be a simple approach to a problem that has plagued the American shipbuilding industry for two decades, it is nevertheless one that moves toward remedies advocated by both sides.

---

[27] Naval officials have made no categorical statement on the number of yards or capacity needed as a mobilization base for fleet requirements. Recent testimony implies that the present capability is probably sufficient. The Department of Commerce, however, has concluded that the current shipbuilding base is insufficient for building merchant ships in a sustained conflict. The four-volume *Report of Commission on American Shipbuilding to the President of the U.S. and Congress of the United States* (Washington, D.C.: U.S. Government Printing Office, October 1973) supports the Department of Commerce estimate.

9

ISSUES AND PROBLEMS

This chapter summarizes and comments on some of the major issues and problems facing managers of defense transportation. Many of these problems require decisions at policy levels within the Department of Defense and the Maritime Administration, and some can be handled effectively only with guidance from Congress. An issue may be defined as a question that has elicited two or more identifiable and generally incompatible points of view. A problem may be defined as implying not opposing viewpoints, but rather a general agreement among the interested parties that some form of corrective action is needed. As a rule, opinions are not yet set, and the parties are willing to consider all proposed solutions.

Issues

Does DOD require a nucleus fleet of commercial-type ships in peacetime? The 1954 Wilson-Weeks agreement sets down DOD's "right" to have such a fleet. Over the years, this prerogative has been justified and defended by Defense and Military Sealift Command officials. On the other hand, in 1971, Maritime Administrator Andrew Gibson questioned DOD's need to maintain such a capability. His position was that the merchant marine was entirely capable of meeting all DOD peacetime shipping requirements, a view taken generally by the Maritime Administration and industry representatives. DOD justifies maintaining its own small peacetime merchant marine by claiming a need for readily available shipping in a contingency. The implication is that privately owned shipping could not meet this need.

The key question is not whether DOD-owned shipping will

always be quickly available. It will not.[1] The real question is whether privately owned ships can be made available within the time prescribed by DOD planners. An important consideration is the disposition of American shipping on any given day. Typically between 90 and 100 general-cargo ships will be found in East, Gulf, and West Coast ports. If only one-quarter of this shipping were available for call-up, it would exceed in numbers and tonnage the entire MSC dry-cargo nucleus fleet. Other considerations, however, are relevant. First, is this the type of shipping preferred by DOD? Not necessarily, since many of these ships will be containerships. This poses the question whether containerships can be made acceptable. In short, they can and they must, since it is projected that over half the U.S.-flag dry-cargo fleet will be of this type within the next ten years.

Other considerations are: Would union crews sail the ships? Would the companies make the ships available? There is no evidence of reluctance among crews to sail into combat areas. The record of Vietnam and Korea is conclusive in this respect.[2] Owners would be willing to make their ships available with an agreement assuring equitable compensation for the time the vessels are in military service and for any other identifiable losses. Given such an agreement, there is no reason to suppose that sufficient numbers of ships would not be quickly made available should a contingency occur.

Should more DOD air cargo be allocated to private carriers? The primary consideration is whether the private carriers could meet all DOD airlift requirements. Because there is no equivalent of the C-5A in the private sector, the answer for the present must be negative. For this reason, the Military Airlift Command differs from its sister agency, MSC, since commercial and MSC-owned sealift assets are substitutable. There is, however, no present substitute for the C-5A.[3]

Another consideration influencing any DOD allocation decision will be the importance attached to seeing the DOD-proposed airlift enhancement program realized. It is difficult to visualize Congress

---

[1] MSC nucleus shipping, like commercial shipping, is dispersed worldwide. It was not available in the Israeli contingency, and it probably could not return to ports in the continental United States and be ready to load any faster than commercial shipping. A distinct advantage in relying on commercial shipping is that a sufficient number of ships are always in continental U.S. ports, which cannot be said for the much smaller nucleus fleet.

[2] There were isolated examples of crews refusing to sail to ports in Vietnam, but they are no more typical than some of the highly publicized recent "mutinies" on navy capital ships.

[3] This will not necessarily be true in the future. See Chapter 5, particularly on the purpose of Project INTACT and forecasts of the long-term growth in air freight.

approving a full-fledged program, with the likelihood of an attendant operational subsidy, without the active support of industry. The trade-off might well take the form of industry support for an air enhancement program in return for a greater share of DOD air freight. Whether Congress would support the air enhancement program under these circumstances is an open question. If the tone of the hearings on the allocation of DOD cargo between MAC and private carriers is any guide, the allocation question would almost certainly weigh heavily in the final decision.

There is not enough air cargo, military and commercial, to employ the full capacity of both MAC and civil airlift systems. Except for the C-5A, MAC's aircraft are in the same situation as MSC's nucleus shipping, that is, industry and military resources in general may be substituted for each other. With the airline industry in a depressed state in 1975 and with U.S. overseas military commitments reduced, a choice may eventually have to be made between MAC grounding some C-130s and C-141s and the civil sector laying up a part of its air freight or freight-convertible inventory.

If it is held to be more cost-effective to move DOD air cargo by commercial planes, with a consequent lay-up of some MAC planes, then the viability of the CRAF agreement becomes considerably more important. Can and will the private sector respond in a contingency? There has never been any suggestion that the airlines would not fully honor their commitments in a call-up. On the other hand, the CRAF agreement has never been implemented. And clouding the issue still more was the airlines' reluctance to commit aircraft voluntarily to the 1973 Israeli resupply effort.[4] If significantly more DOD air cargo is moved in commercial planes and MAC's airlift is reduced, the CRAF agreement should clarify each side's responsibilities in Israeli-type situations. Such a clarification should not pose any insurmountable problems.

Should Section 22 be limited to times of national emergency? Most in industry urge repeal or modification of Section 22 of the Act to Regulate Commerce. They say lower rates induced by this section subsidize defense freight. On the other hand, DOD sees Section 22 as a means of saving transportation costs. The Hoover Commission Task Force on Transportation recommended that Section 22 be amended by eliminating authorization for the movement of government freight and passengers at reduced rates. The full commission,

---

[4] The Israeli crisis might have been a good time to have implemented CRAF and the Sealift Readiness Program, if only to demonstrate that the agreements could be counted on in a contingency.

however, declined to recommend the amendment, contenting itself with recognition of "the many cogent reasons for the recommendation."[5] There is truth on both sides. While DOD does not account for a large proportion of carrier revenues, it is nonetheless a very large shipper. Historically, it has not been above using a monopsonist's prerogatives to achieve the lowest possible costs, notwithstanding the oft-made assertion that rates are mutually and voluntarily agreed upon. On the other hand, GAO's findings that DOD payments for rail and highway transportation services are compensatory cannot be ignored. The question raised in Chapter 6 still seems to have merit, that is, Are DOD's savings really a saving at a time when another agency of the federal government is spending billions to restructure and revitalize a large chunk of the nation's rail network? Nor can the billions already spent on the country's highway system be ignored. One solution, admittedly tongue-in-cheek, might be for DOD to retain the estimated $250 million annual saving realized from Section 22, but to pay a fair share of the cost of maintaining a continental U.S. transportation system.

Should privately operated, union-manned merchant ships be assigned an underway replenishment role? The navy has already assigned a good part of its underway replenishment mission to MSC nucleus ships, particularly tankers, manned by civil service crews. Navy justification has been the savings in money and personnel. As yet, however, no privately operated merchant ship has been contracted to perform such a service. The issue cannot forever be ignored, particularly after tests such as *Erna Elizabeth* and *Lash Italia* have demonstrated the feasibility of using merchant ships. Presumably steamship operators would be willing to commit their vessels, and maritime union leadership is already on record as favoring the role. Tanker owners and union leaders in particular can be expected to press their case with the navy, the more so if the depressed tanker market continues.

There well may be valid reasons why merchant ships cannot fulfill some underway replenishment roles effectively, but only experience can finally settle the issue. It would do little harm, and perhaps a great deal of good, for the navy to utilize several union-manned merchant ships in a trial program. As matters stand, suspicion persists that, in denying an underway replenishment role to the merchant marine, the navy is merely "propping up" the Military Sealift Command.

---

[5] Commission on Organization of the Executive Branch of Government, *Transportation*, p. 95.

Is a national defense reserve fleet necessary? The portion of the NDRF retained for national defense is considered old and worn out, mainly because of neglect. The Maritime Administration has allocated about 1 percent of its authorized budget to maintain the NDRF. Navy spokesmen claim these ships could not be broken out quickly enough in a contingency. Industry and union spokesmen have had few kind words for the aging ships that make up the fleet, but none of these comments have directly addressed the concept of an NDRF. The main concern was with the physical condition of the fleet.[6] The single exception was the passage of the so-called Mariner Bill in 1974, an effort by Congress to renew the fleet by adding newer ships in a trade-in and scrap exchange. Yet the concept of a reserve merchant fleet remains very much alive. Defense officials have recognized the need for back-up shipping, the more so because finding work for an active DOD-controlled fleet became increasingly difficult. Proposals are under consideration to upgrade a certain number of Victory ships at the three NDRF sites, so they can be broken out quickly. Another idea is to create a smaller ready reserve of 1960-vintage break-bulk ships, which would constitute a ready reserve force under MSC control.

In their haste to make up for earlier neglect, however, agencies and officials risked proposing solutions that were less than cost-efficient. One approach worth considering would be to place newer break-bulk ships acquired by the government for contingency operations in the custody of steamship operators. These ships could be maintained by them, at their facilities, under a government contract similar in scope to the general agency agreements under which private firms operated government-owned ships in the Korean and Vietnam conflicts. Drydock work would be arranged by the companies, as would all the other prescribed maintenance necessary to keep the ships in a ready state. Upgraded Victory ships probably could be left more efficiently in the care of the Maritime Administration.

There are three reasons for turning over this government function to the private sector. First, the ships of any future NDRF will most likely be ships such as U.S. Lines Challenger class vessels or Lykes Brothers Gulf Andes and Gulf Pride class ships. What better home could be found than with their original owners, who know them best? Second, it would be an efficient and practical way of increasing the cash flow to firms in an industry whose earnings are

---

[6] One question worthy of research is: How long can a laid up ship be preserved effectively? The average age of an NDRF Victory ship exceeds thirty years, but most have been operated for only about ten years. Good data on this could be important in planning the future of the NDRF.

historically cyclical and often negative. It should not be hard to arrive at an agreement that is equitable to all parties, with an overall savings to the federal government. Finally, the ships would in all likelihood be maintained at sites along the East, Gulf, and Pacific coasts. These mini-reserve fleets, of from two to ten vessels each, would be in a good position to move either to a loading berth or to a shipyard.[7]

Who shall educate tomorrow's merchant marine officer and provide the training necessary to make the merchant marine truly a naval auxiliary? This is not a compelling issue, but enough questions have been raised to warrant a brief examination. One of the more important questions is, What agencies can educate tomorrow's merchant marine officers most efficiently? There are three possibilities: the federal academy at Kings Point, the six state maritime schools, and union-operated schools for candidates with experience at sea. Federal support for Kings Point and state schools is approximately $15 million annually, but no federal or state funds support the union schools.

Too many officers are being turned out for the jobs available, Maritime Administration projections notwithstanding. Moreover, this education is not provided in the most efficient way. State academies, like all institutions of higher education, are under severe financial pressures, and without a large increase in federal aid, some or all may have to close. It is considerably cheaper for the federal government to provide a four-year education at a state school. One estimate is that the cost to the federal government for a state academy graduate is $5,000 compared with $19,000 for his Kings Point counterpart.[8]

A debate at the annual American Merchant Marine Conference in 1954 is as relevant today as then. R. D. Sweeney, a supporter of state maritime academies, questioned the justification of a federal role in maritime education:

> I presume that in the federal government there are, perhaps, more lawyers and more doctors employed by the government than there are officers in the United States merchant marine. Do you feel that the federal government should start a college for doctors and a college for lawyers? . . .

---

[7] A steamship contractor might face two problems in maintaining NDRF ships: (1) finding a predominantly fresh-water anchorage (marine growth on hulls is less of a problem in fresh water); and (2) obtaining low-cost wharfage near major seaports, should it prove to be more practical to maintain custodial ships alongside. In the opinion of steamship-company officials, neither problem invalidates the concept. The government might acquire these ships by having the Maritime Administration take title to them and allowing the market value to be credited toward construction of new tonnage by the original owners for operation under the American flag—as in the earlier "trade in and build" program.

[8] Hayler, *U.S. Naval Institute Proceedings*, p. 53.

Our constitution is one of delegated powers to the states, and the states do not delegate to the federal government the right of education. I do not know whether you agree with that, but it is a fact. Therefore, it would not appear to be a federal function to train these people for private industry. I believe you will agree the merchant marine is a private industry. I am getting down to fundamentals of government and not economics.[9]

What makes this twenty-year-old comment relevant today is the debate about a Uniformed Services University of the Health Sciences, that is, a military medical school. Public Law 92-246, passed in 1972, established the school, but since then the Defense Manpower Commission has recommended against its being funded. The commission estimated the cost per graduate could reach $200,000, or more than five times the amount it would cost to train a military doctor by awarding a scholarship at a civil medical school.

Another consideration is, Who will provide merchant seamen and officers with the skills necessary to perform navy underway replenishment requirements? If the merchant marine is to become a true naval auxiliary, such training is essential.[10] Alternatives include navy-run schools or courses, Maritime Administration schools, and training by the unions. Since the merchant marine is a private industry, the most logical way would seem to be training by maritime unions, perhaps initially funded with federal "seed" money.

How shall DOD procure its peacetime sealift and airlift needs? The controversy centers on how MSC procures its sealift. Its modified competitive bid method is considered by the Maritime Administration, the Federal Maritime Commission, and most of the private operators to be detrimental to the long-run financial stability of the companies. Most industry spokesmen favor a system similar to DOD procurement of commercial airlift. At a minimum, the Maritime Administration would revise the bid system so that all firms bidding would receive some cargo, with the low bidder receiving the larger share. This proposal was rejected by the secretary of defense in 1975.

Since DOD airlift cargo is allocated to airlines on a nonbid basis, why not procure sealift by this method? DOD soon may face hard choices on how its cargo should move to overseas points—by sea or by air. Before comparisons of cost effectiveness can be made, a common method of procurement for both modes is needed.

---

[9] "Discussion," *Proceedings of American Merchant Marine Conference*, vol. 20 (December 1954), p. 64.

[10] Papers certifying underway replenishment proficiency could be issued by the U.S. Coast Guard in the same manner it certifies other shipboard skills.

The point made in considering Section 22 rates applies here as well. It makes little sense to achieve a DOD "savings" at the expense of the financial health of the shipping industry. A bidding procedure may separate the efficient firm from the inefficient, but in the long run it may also decrease the merchant shipping mobilization base. DOD spokesmen assert that the "total number of ships available [is] considered to be only marginally adequate to meet deployment and resupply objectives" in the event of a war in Europe.[11] The question is, What is the most efficient way to provide federal funds to an industry that is not only essential to national security but also one that cannot exist without federal aid? Wringing out a DOD saving by insisting on a bidding procedure that most in the industry consider cutthroat hardly seems the best way.

How shall naval construction and repair work be apportioned to private and naval shipyards? As indicated in Chapter 8, there is simply not enough conversion, alteration, and repair work to go around. This insufficiency causes many yards, both naval and private, to operate at considerably less than optimum points on their average-cost curves. One approach would be to determine how far private yards can meet the chief of naval operations' strategic and operational requirements and to proceed from there, viewing the naval yards as a back-up capability both for new construction and for CAR work. After this was done, sufficient work would be mandated to the naval yards to insure their operation at close to optimum efficiency. This approach probably would result in the closing of some naval yards, but the probability of that occurring in any case is quite high.

Problems

A number of situations in defense transportation have been defined here as problems rather than issues because by and large contending viewpoints about them have failed to emerge. Six of them are considered.

Optimally equipping U.S.-flag merchant ships to serve as naval auxiliaries. It cannot be said that our merchant marine is optimally equipped to perform the naval auxiliary functions envisioned by framers of the Merchant Marine Act of 1936. The national defense features program has not been sufficiently funded, and administration of the program has been fragmented. Since money for the pro-

---

[11] Bennett, testimony before House Subcommittee on Merchant Marine, June 5, 1975.

gram is included in construction differential subsidy funds, and since the budget is limited, this can easily become a choice between more ships and a lesser number of ships equipped with defense features. It appears advisable to make national defense features funds a line item in either the navy's or Maritime Administration's budget. Congress could then consider national defense features funding independently.

There was also a question about what type of ship qualifies as having a national defense purpose. Navy and Maritime Administration opinion has been divided on the question. The navy sees no national defense purpose for either the large liquid natural gas carriers or the supertankers. Presumably the ships are too large relative to their speed, that is, the possibility of their surviving hostile action is rated too low by the navy. Such reasoning, however, seems simplistic. A supertanker lost at sea may be equivalent to the loss of a fleet of smaller tankers, but it must also be recognized that an entire convoy of smaller tankers could be taken out with only one medium-size atomic weapon.[12] One large ship might be protected more cheaply than thirty smaller ones. The question deserves attention if for no other reason than that Congress appropriates between $20 million and $60 million of public money (construction differential funds) for each liquid natural gas carrier or supertanker built for American flag registry.

Creating a Merchant Marine Naval Reserve. A related consideration is, Can some regular naval reserve forces be used to support the merchant marine during an emergency? The Merchant Marine Naval Reserve program has been something less than an unqualified success since the Congress legislated it in the Merchant Marine Act of 1936. No one reason for this lack of success can be singled out. Merchant marine officer unions have been only lukewarm to the concept, and, if the navy considers the program essential, it has yet to make a case at appropriations hearings. Nor has the Maritime Administration espoused the cause over the years. Yet it is the intent of Congress that the United States have a strong merchant marine reserve program. If war should come tomorrow, it will be the merchant marine officers aboard our multimillion dollar ships today who will be entrusted with fulfilling the vessel's assigned task. There will be precious little time for them to learn the latest navy convoy doctrine and communications procedure and how best to secure the ship against chemical, biological, or radiological attack. No other naval reserve program

---

[12] This, of course, would depend on the convoy formation, that is, spread out, in line, or clustered.

is more important than the Merchant Marine Naval Reserve. Unfortunately, it has received the least attention.

Naval reserve efforts in support of the Reserve Merchant Ship Defense System are commendable, though the navy had to be coaxed by Congress into giving it a trial. Under this program, naval air reservists would fly anti-submarine warfare helicopters from containerships. Reserve helicopter squadrons could be deployed aboard container (and perhaps other) cargo-type ships in a matter of hours, thereby giving some protection to the ship or convoy. Other ideas for using regular naval reserve forces in support of the merchant marine can be expected and should be encouraged.

Obtaining privately owned ships and aircraft in a nonmobilization contingency. Programs like the Sealift Readiness Program and the Civil Reserve Air Fleet are predicated on the assumption that there will always be enough DOD cargo movement to insure private-carrier participation. These programs depend upon the carriers' desire to carry defense cargoes, which will make him willing to pre-pledge part of his assets for use in a contingency. But there may come a time when defense cargoes are too small to be attractive. In the case of sealift, cargo moved overseas has already declined from a Vietnam high of 28 million measurement tons to a present total of 10 million measurement tons, and it could drop even lower. All vessels receiving an operating-differential subsidy might be required to commit vessels to the Sealift Readiness Program, but other vessels would remain exempt. Moreover, subsidized firms are probably under enough operating constraints already, and any more could become self-defeating. In this regard, at what point would an operator decide to go out of business or to transfer his vessels to a foreign flag? The program that is adopted should impact equally on all carriers in a particular mode and be as uniform as possible between modes. This requirement will become increasingly important as movement by air and sea become more nearly substitutable, perhaps in the near future.[13]

Using an intermodal transportation system in a contingency or mobilization. The chief problem areas center on the container mode. How to unload non-self-sustaining containerships across a beach is one problem. Whether to maintain a DOD inventory of container-support equipment essential in a mobilization, but of limited use in peacetime, is another. Equipment essential to mobilization would include flat rack containers and lighters to move containers from the

---

[13] Sealift has enjoyed a tremendous ton-mile cost advantage over airlift. With the development of air-container movement and a new generation of all-freight aircraft, this advantage can be expected to diminish significantly.

ship to the beach.[14] Other container-related problems, discussed in Chapter 7, include the development of a means to transport ammunition safely in civilian containers and obtaining enough containers quickly in a contingency.[15] All of these problems are being addressed by the Department of Defense, but the solutions cost money and Congress has often been hostile to increased defense spending. Nevertheless, sufficient funds should be requested and appropriated to purchase 15,000 flat racks. In the past Congress has insisted that DOD be cost-conscious in hardware purchases. Stockpiling hardware items that may never be used is not an easy decision, particularly with so many other demands for funds. This purchase, however, is essential if the United States is to use its merchant marine fully in a contingency or mobilization. In this case, a large military expenditure is required to insure optimal use of a civilian transportation asset, that is, a fleet of containerships that will probably approach a $10 billion investment by 1985.

Smoothing the rough edges of the DOD-private transportation interface. It is widely accepted that DOD has no choice but to rely on commercial transportation in peacetime, wartime, or a contingency. This is a point that defense officials continually stress, and make a virtue, in testimony before Congress. The rougher edges of this interface were identified and discussed earlier, and only one additional observation need be made here.[16] The testimony and writings of defense and industry spokesmen over the years indicate clearly that defense officials are fully conversant with defense matters, and industry spokesmen with industry matters, but neither fully understands the day-to-day operations and problems of the other. If that shortcoming could be corrected, benefits to all would be significant. One approach might be an industry–defense personnel exchange. Senior MSC officials might be given six-month temporary duty as assistants to presidents of steamship firms, and senior company officials could profit from a "tour of duty" at the Pentagon. The same case can be made for exchanges between labor union and defense

---

[14] Another technique with some promise of commercial application is lifting containers ashore with a heliballoon, a helium-filled balloon propelled by turboprop engines mounted on rotating wings. For a good nontechnical description, see "Supersize Airlifter," *Mechanix Illustrated*, January 1976, pp. 44–46.

[15] Whether the 75,000 CONEX containers in the DOD inventory could be of some use in a contingency might be worth considering. At present, most are being used for storage.

[16] In Chapter 7, it was noted that the army is developing a microwave scanner to read container labels on MILVANS more efficiently. Exploring commercial application of the scanner and its cost, efficiency, and adaptability to commercial markings could provide opportunities for DOD-industry cooperation.

officials.[17] If an intern program is not feasible, then scheduled and continuing exchange seminars could be run. Industry–defense contacts have been limited to occasional presentations before professional associations with a common membership, but much more dialogue is needed.

Supplementing and protecting U.S. merchant shipping during hostilities. In a NATO war, U.S.-flag shipping by itself would be insufficient to deploy American forces to Europe. This was acknowledged by the secretary of defense in his FY 1975 annual report when he announced that the NATO allies had agreed to make available some 300 merchant ships in the event of a mobilization.[18] These ships would become available only at the time a mobilization was ordered, however, and not before. Moreover, they would not be called if sufficient U.S.-flag shipping were available.

While this joint U.S.-European effort appears favorable, problems could arise. First, a deployment of American forces to Europe might be ordered in the hope of preventing a war, not starting one. Mobilization of U.S. forces is a significant step up the escalation ladder and one that probably would not be taken immediately. Rather, in the beginning at least, American forces would probably be deployed without a mobilization taking place. Under the agreement with our European allies, the initial (and perhaps entire) effort would be carried out by American-flag shipping. The possible inequity is apparent—in a deployment without mobilization, American ships could be called up under the Sealift Readiness Program or some similar arrangement, and taken from their trades, while European shipping carried on business as usual.[19] The possibility is one that Congress might consider.

Assuming a deployment does take place, and that the sealift responsibility is primarily American, protecting this shipping becomes

---

[17] Industry, academia, and government agencies already exchange management-level personnel. Government-academic exchanges include the American Association of Collegiate Schools of Business—Sears Roebuck Faculty Fellows Program and the U.S. General Accounting Office Faculty Fellow Program. An industry-government example is the Federal Executive Exchange Program. There are also a number of congressional fellowship programs and the White House Fellows Program.

[18] Department of Defense, *Annual Defense Department Report for FY 1975*, p. 166.

[19] A question might be raised about the emergency role of the Effective United States Controlled Fleet, American-owned ships operating under foreign flag. This study simply accepts the stated position of Norman Polmar that "their availability to support U.S. foreign policy goals in time of peace or carry combat loads in wartime is highly speculative." See Norman Polmar, *Soviet Naval Challenge for the 1970s* (New York: Crane, Russak & Co., 1974), p. 78.

an urgent matter. Defense equipping of merchant ships was discussed in Chapter 3, as was deploying naval reserve helicopter squadrons aboard containerships. Any defense equipping effort should be co-ordinated closely with efforts to outfit new merchant ships optimally with national defense features. These features should be a line item in either the Maritime Administration or the navy budget. Alternatively, defense-equipping and the defense-feature appropriations might be combined into a single line item.

There is a question whether U.S. shipping would be allowed to cross the Atlantic without hindrance prior to a European war breaking out. If a massive American deployment were undertaken, would the Soviet Navy, particularly its submarines, allow this shipping to pass through? Those who say an attack on U.S. shipping would auto-matically result in hostilities should be reminded that such attacks did take place on U.S. ships prior to U.S. entry into World War II, and hostilities did not automatically follow.[20]

Conclusion

This chapter has focused on some of the problems and issues that defense transportation managers will face in the future. The comments have suggested that the United States can no longer maintain parallel military transportation capabilities when the private sector can do the job. It is recognized that, in a greater reliance on privately operated transportation, greater risks will be entailed. But risks have been accepted in procuring (or not procuring) certain weapon systems, as well as in the SALT accords. The list of weapons and weapons systems that Congress has scrubbed is a lengthy one. The judgment has been that the United States simply cannot afford to cover all bets—exactly the point being made here. If more civilian resources can be put into the defense transportation system, then, that should be done for reasons of economy. But, as stated in Chapter 1, if such a sub-stitution imperils (and not merely inconveniences) strategic mobility, then the defense asset must remain. Congress must decide.

Some of the problems discussed will probably require new legis-

---

[20] If American shipping could safely be used in a U.S. deployment to Europe, the possibility of utilizing the S.S. *United States* might merit a reexamination. The ship is a part of the NDRF and is laid up at Norfolk, Va. The vessel could be converted to a troop carrier at an estimated cost of $15 million. Based on the troop-carrying capabilities of Cunard Lines' *Queen Mary* and *Queen Elizabeth* in World War II, the *United States* probably could transport 12,000 to 15,000 troops to Europe in about three-and-one-half days. If the actual cost were even three times the estimate, it would still seem a partial alternative to the $6.8 billion Air Enhancement Program.

lation. Some prerogatives of private management will undoubtedly be constrained. If the private sector chooses to become an effective part of DOD's defense transportation system, then it should understand that contingency and mobilization requirements must be planned on the certainty—rather than the likelihood—that resources will be available when needed. In this respect, a page could profitably be taken from the Israeli book. The point can be made thus. Perhaps section (b) of the preamble to the Merchant Marine Act of 1936 should be amended by inserting a single word. Instead of requiring a merchant marine "capable of serving as a naval and military auxiliary in time of war or national emergency," the section might read "in time of *peace*, war, or national emergency." That would say it all. The point would apply equally to all transport modes.

10
MANAGING DEFENSE TRANSPORTATION

This study has examined the defense transportation system and concludes that the day of a significant DOD in-house transportation capability is drawing to a close. Although DOD steadfastly and correctly maintains it is largely dependent on commercial transportation assets, it must be prepared to become even more so. There is simply no alternative under the tight defense budgets of recent years. Complete or almost complete reliance upon privately operated transportation resources would entail some risk, but policy makers have accepted risks in other areas. Calculating probabilities in national security management, when it is accepted that all possibilities cannot be covered, has been standard procedure for a long time.

Although in-house DOD transportation may be ending, the management of defense transportation is not. If anything, it will become even more important. Management responsibilities on the supply side, such as managing DOD-owned sea and air assets, will decrease, but managing the demand for defense transportation must continue. And managing this demand in an increasingly complex intermodal environment will be no small undertaking.

The Coming Environment

At present, the U.S. transportation system is fragmented. Railroads, airlines, trucking firms, inland waterway operators, and ocean steamship firms are not combined within a single corporation because present legislation prohibits horizontal integration of transportation services. In the past few years, however, efforts to achieve significant deregulation in all transportation sectors have intensified. The Nixon and Ford administrations have made far-reaching proposals, and there is considerable sentiment in Congress for less government interference in the private transportation sector. Academic economists, once almost totally committed to regulation, are now among those most vocally opposed to its continuation.[1] Corporate leaders recommend not only less regulation per se but also repeal of laws that would prevent mergers and acquisitions between the various transport modes.[2]

Management of private transportation is fragmented, but responsibility for regulation of the industry is even more so. Among the independent regulatory bodies, the Interstate Commerce Commission regulates railroads, trucking, pipelines, and waterways; the Civil Aeronautics Board regulates the airlines; and the Federal Maritime Commission, the ocean carriers. In the executive department, the Maritime Administration of the Department of Commerce is the promotional agency for the merchant marine, while the Department of Transportation has an overall coordinative function as well as responsibility for transportation safety.

On the legislative side, Congress has somewhat fewer committees to cover a greater number of modes, but no single committee in either house is responsible for all transportation legislation. On the other hand, if the oversight of defense transportation is included in the general transportation category, congressional responsibility is as fragmented as that of industry or the regulatory agencies.

A change in this transportation environment seems highly likely. Many higher transportation costs are attributed to inefficiencies caused by regulation. Economic losses from ICC regulation in 1968 alone were estimated at $3.8 billion, and may have been as much as $8.8 billion.[3]

Other forces motivating change include the increasing use of intermodal containers and the high cost of energy. Criticisms of the U.S. transportation system are becoming more frequent. In 1970, prior to the energy crisis, at the behest of the Departments of Commerce and Defense, the National Academy of Sciences undertook a study of legal impediments to international intermodal transporta-

---

[1] See Thomas G. Moore, *Freight Transportation Regulation* (Washington, D.C.: American Enterprise Institute, 1972) and James C. Miller, editor, *Perspectives on Federal Transportation Policy* (Washington, D.C.: American Enterprise Institute, 1975).

[2] W. Graham Claytor, Jr., *The Future of American Railroads*, a 1974 taped address to transportation students of Clemson University, Taped Addresses of American Industrial Leaders, Sirrine Library, Clemson University, Clemson, South Carolina. See also "Trucks, Trains, Planes, Boats, All in One Company?" *U.S. News and World Report*, September 25, 1967, pp. 118–120.

[3] Moore, *Freight Transportation Regulation*, p. 80.

tion.[4] Although the study was to focus on through rates, through documentation, and through liability, it pointed out that at the time a national transportation policy existed in name only. Objectives set forth in a statement of national transportation policy in 1940 and goals established in the creation of a Department of Transportation in 1967 had not been achieved.[5] In a wide-ranging critique of U.S. transportation, Representative Brock Adams (Democrat, Washington) stated:

> Physically, the United States has what is potentially the world's most efficient network of highways, airways, railroads and canals. But because of the way government regulates this network, its components don't add up to a system at all, but rather to a giant free-for-all. Among the rules employed by government regulators to referee this free-for-all, preserving the status quo comes first, and enforcing efficiency last.[6]

These and countless other charges have not been without impact. Today there is serious consideration of the possibility of combining the FMC, ICC, and CAB into a single board. In 1975, a member of the ICC suggested that the ICC and the FMC might be merged as a first step.[7]

Thus, a markedly different transportation environment is a reasonable forecast. The same forces that compel DOD to utilize commercial transportation as a cost-effective expedient also compel the nation to reassess how its transportation is managed and regulated. In the 1960s, *U.S. News and World Report* prophesied: "A new type of company may soon be taking shape in this country—the transportation company offering all services: rail, truck, air, water. Its aim: faster, cheaper passage for goods and people across the continent and across the ocean."[8] How DOD transportation management will interface with this new transportation company and a new transportation environment is a topic of immense importance.

---

[4] National Research Council, *Legal Impediments to International Intermodal Transportation: Selected Problems, Options, and Recommended Solutions* (Washington, D.C.: National Academy of Sciences, 1971).

[5] The Transportation Act of 1940 called for the development, coordination, and preservation of a national transportation system. The act establishing a Department of Transportation declared that one purpose of the new agency would be to develop and improve a coordinated transportation service.

[6] Brock Adams, "The Shameful State of Transport," *Reader's Digest*, February 1975, pp. 61–66.

[7] *Washington Star-News*, January 15, 1975, p. A-21.

[8] "Trucks, Trains, Planes, Boats, All in One Company?" *U.S. News and World Report*, pp. 118–120.

Present Management of DOD Transportation

The Defense Transportation System consists of military-controlled terminal facilities, MAC-controlled airlift, Military Sealift Command-controlled or arranged sealift, and government-owned or controlled air or land transportation.[9] This system is operated and managed by the air force, army, and navy. Transportation logistics is a service function, rather than a function of the office of the secretary of defense. That logistics should remain a service responsibility is an article of faith among all the services. As one old defense hand put it, "Armed forces unification took away the power of the services to prepare for and make war. What was left was the logistics responsibility. They guard it jealously and won't give it up without a fight. It is really all that they have left."[10]

Although the defense transportation system as defined is primarily a management responsibility of the services, defense transportation in general is more pervasive. DOD owns and leases commercial containers, and, as noted earlier, overseeing the development of a DOD-wide container distribution system is a responsibility of the assistant secretary of defense for installations and logistics. And, while MSC has responsibility for a part of the navy's underway replenishment mission, a part remains with the Naval Sea Systems Command under the chief of naval operations. Also, private industry interfaces with the military at many points within DOD apart from strictly service contacts, just as the military interfaces with other government agencies. Thus, transportation logistics may be a responsibility of the single managers for airlift, sealift, and land transportation, but their responsibility is not complete.

Two previous questions may be reconsidered in the context of efficiently managing DOD transport: How can a DOD-wide container distribution system be achieved? and How can a shrinking amount of DOD cargo be apportioned between airlift and sealift? If the first problem were solved, and a DOD-wide intermodal distribution system were in place, who would control and assign cargo entering this system? Would it be the responsibility of the services as is now gen-

---

[9] W. D. Gaddis, "Logistics and the Future of Navy Transportation," *Defense Management Journal*, April 1975, p. 24.

[10] Prior to leaving office as secretary of the army, Howard H. Callaway said, "If I wanted to go down in the tank today, this building would explode." (The tank is the top secret room where the joint chiefs of staff plan military operations.) Despite the tradition that the military operates under civilian control, under present law service secretaries are not included in operation decisions. When Robert C. Seamans was secretary of the air force, for example, the Christmas bombings of Hanoi were conducted without his knowledge. See *Greenville News* (South Carolina), July 3, 1975, p. 18.

erally the case? Military departments insist that each service must control its own air-eligible cargo entering the military airlift system. It simply does not follow that if a well-conceived intermodal container distribution system were in place, it would be optimally used, particularly in view of the problem of apportioning DOD cargo between airlift and sealift. How are DOD airlift and sealift resources to be exercised when the total cargo moved is decreasing? Would the air force specify that the long leg of its cargo movement be by air in order to utilize MAC planes when, in fact, sealift would be more cost-effective? Or would some cargo move by sea that truly could have been efficiently moved by air?[11]

Finally, can the present service managers of military transportation deal effectively and efficiently with a truly intermodal private transportation company? DOD may be dealing with a firm that is no longer dependent upon a single mode as a source of its revenues. To such a firm, DOD use of Section 22 rates will be less important, as will DOD procurement practices. The contracting parties will be more evenly matched, and some firms may well forgo carrying defense cargo. In deciding whether to pledge its planes and ships under a CRAF or Sealift Readiness Program in return for qualifying as a defense cargo carrier, the large intermodal firm will be able to weigh costs and benefits with more sagacity.

The implication so far has been that, in the intermodal transportation world of tomorrow, DOD will probably be dependent on the private sector for its entire transportation needs.[12] It has been previously implied that defense transportation management responsibilities should be lodged in one place. That implication is now made explicit.

Attempts to Combine Functions. The idea of combining DOD transportation management functions is not new. It has been recommended by several prestigious groups and panels. The Transportation Task Force of the Hoover Commission recommended that an assistant secretary of defense for transportation be created to oversee DOD transportation functions. The commission did not agree but did make this recommendation:

---

[11] This problem is addressed from the air force point of view in a study by Lionel A. Boudreaux and Thomas J. Cooper, "A Comparaive Analysis of the Relationships of Total Distribution Costs Between Airlift and Sealift," unpublished Master's thesis, School of Systems and Logistics, Air Force Institute of Technology, 1974.

[12] At present this is not conceded in the Department of Defense. See Paul H. Riley, "DOD Transportation: Management Problems and the Search for Solutions," *Defense Transportation Journal* (December 1975), pp. 6–14.

That the Secretary of Defense establish a Director of Transportation having no responsibilities except those pertaining to traffic and transportation. He should have all necessary authority to direct the traffic management activities, passenger and freight, in all the Military Services, including the coordination and consolidation of functions and facilities, to the extent that his office determines it to be necessary and practicable. He should report to and be subject only to the overriding authority of the Assistant Secretary of Defense for Supply and Logistics.[13]

Among the duties recommended for the director of transportation were to prescribe routing policy to be observed by all services, and to prescribe policy to be followed in the distribution of passenger and freight traffic among carriers.[14]

Fifteen years later the Blue Ribbon Defense Panel recommended:

The responsibility for providing supply distribution, maintenance and transportation services to the combatant forces in Unified and Specified Commands under the Strategic and Tactical Commands should be assigned to the unified Logistics Command. The Logistics Command should be assigned the traffic management and terminal management functions now allocated to the Military Traffic Management and Terminal Service (MTMTS), the Military Sea Transportation Service (MSTS) and the Theater Traffic Management agencies. The Military Airlift Command and Military Sea Transportation Command both should be assigned to the Logistics Command. The Logistics Command should be directed to develop, under policy guidance of the Assistant Secretary of Defense (Telecommunications), an ADP logistics system to encompass supply distribution elements that can be shared among the Services, and all development and procurement activity toward separate ADP logistics systems not essential to support of near-term operations should be suspended.[15]

Partially in response to the Blue Ribbon recommendation, the deputy secretary of defense issued a directive on February 24, 1971, that transferred the functions of the Military Sealift Command to the Military Traffic Management and Terminal Service. Included in the functions to be transferred was the procurement of ocean shipping.

---

[13] Commission on Organization of the Executive Branch of Government, *Transportation*, p. 63.

[14] Commission on Organization of the Executive Branch of Government, *Transportation*, p. 64.

[15] Blue Ribbon Defense Panel, *Report to the President and the Secretary of Defense*, p. 107.

The Special Subcommittee on Transportation of the House Committee on Armed Services held hearings on the directive in the fall of 1971 and issued its report on November 18, 1971.

As might be expected, army spokesmen supported the directive while the navy opposed it vehemently. Even though the Military Airlift Command was not included in the merger, spokesmen for the air force were asked for their views. The report stated:

> In short, the subcommittee feels that the very items that led to the proposal to transfer procurement functions of MSC to MTMTS could at some time in the not too distant future apply to the Military Airlift Command. For the same reasons that it is important to the Military Airlift Command to retain its procurement responsibility for airlift, it is important to the Military Sealift Command to retain its responsibility for the procurement of sealift.[16]

The subcommittee report strongly favored letting the air force procure airlift, letting MSC procure sealift, and letting MTMTS procure land transportation. On airlift, the report concluded:

> The subcommittee wishes to point out that if the arguments used to support the transfer of Military Sealift Command functions to the Military Traffic Management and Terminal Service were valid, they would apply with the same validity to justify a transfer of similar functions from the Military Airlift Command. The subcommittee is not persuaded by these arguments and therefore is opposed to any such transfer.[17]

Whether the views of the subcommittee were also the views of a majority in the Congress will never be known. The move to combine MSC and MTMTS was handled less adroitly by the office of secretary of defense than any other issue in recent memory. First, the joint chiefs of staff were not consulted before the directive was released, nor were the Armed Services Committees of Congress informed of the proposed transfer. These oversights were fully exploited by the navy.[18] More important, the necessary homework had not been

---

[16] U.S. Congress, House, Special Subcommittee on Transportation of Committee on Armed Services, *Report on Proposed Transfer of Military Sealift Command Functions to Military Traffic Management and Terminal Service*, 92d Cong., 1st sess., November 1971, p. 6935.

[17] House, Special Subcommittee on Transportation of Committee on Armed Services, *Report on Proposed Transfer of MSC Functions to MTMTS*, p. 6838.

[18] The navy argued that its daily contacts with the shipping industry gave it an understanding of merchant marine needs, requirements, and problems. It might be noted that no industry spokesman testified at the hearings, hence the navy position that it understood (or sympathized with) merchant marine problems was not substantiated.

done in the Office of Secretary of Defense. This was apparent from the testimony of those favoring the merger. While leaving MAC out may have been good service politics, it brought the integrity of the proposal into doubt.

Managing Defense Transportation: The Future

Events since 1971 make the establishment of a single DOD manager for transportation even more necessary. Among the changes that have occurred are the following:

(1) The rapid increase in the use of containers for the surface movement of commercial and defense cargo—in the case of DOD cargo, moving from about 50 percent in containers to a figure approaching 80 percent. This movement toward containers is perforce a movement toward intermodal transportation, and the basis of intermodal transportation is the through movement of cargo, without respect to whether it moves by air, land, or sea. The only constraint is that it move as efficiently as possible. Intermodal technology has improved significantly since 1971. Ocean carriers such as Sealand's SL-7 containership, Lykes Brothers' Seabarge class ships, and the large new RO/RO vessels of States and Matson steamship companies are the chief examples with respect to sealift.

(2) The incorporation of airlift, albeit limited, into the intermodal transportation system. In the 1971 hearings it was asserted that it would not be logical to include MAC in the proposed MSC-MTMTS merger. The reasoning was that airlift was unique and by and large not substitutable with respect to surface carriers. In a signed article appearing in late 1975, however, the commander of MAC called for the dynamic development of an all-cargo aircraft. Possible suggested commercial uses of the plane included the movement of grain, coffee crops, automobiles, and manufactured goods.[19]

(3) A significant decrease in the size of the MSC nucleus and chartered fleet. It is one thing to contemplate merging a controlled fleet of over 150 vessels and quite another to merge a fleet that has shrunk to one-third that size.

(4) The rising cost of transportation. In FY 1974, DOD shipped approximately 9 million tons of cargo less than in FY 1973, but the cost remained essentially unchanged. Tight defense budgets necessitate improvement in DOD management of its transportation dollar.

The above changes, as well as others, suggest that the future

---

[19] Paul K. Carlton, "Military Airlift Commander Calls For Dynamic Development of All Cargo Aircraft," *Defense Transportation Journal*, December 1975, p. 32.

will see a much different transportation world than existed at the beginning of the decade. The remaining question is how best to manage defense transportation in this new environment.

Suggestions

(1) The Department of Defense should consider establishing a director of defense transportation to replace the present single managers for airlift, sealift, and land movement. The twenty-year-old Hoover Commission recommendations offer a good departure point.[20]

(2) The Department of Defense should state explicitly that it considers commercial resources the primary component in the defense transportation system and that an organic DOD transportation capability is considered supplementary, to be used only if a demonstrated need can be shown.

(3) Congress should review the need for enabling standby legislation to insure that, in a contingency or mobilization, commercial transportation will be readily available and entirely responsive to Department of Defense needs.[21]

(4) The navy should make explicit its position on the use of privately operated union-manned merchant ships in an underway replenishment role. If its position is negative, the burden of proof should be upon the navy.

(5) In regard to education and reserve forces, the navy should consider increasing its commitment to the Merchant Marine Naval Reserve program. The Maritime Administration should review how best to educate and train tomorrow's merchant marine officer. In anticipation of an underway replenishment role for the merchant marine, it should establish a pilot program to train merchant seamen and offer guidance and assistance to maritime unions.

It would be appropriate to conclude this study with an estimate of savings if DOD relied entirely upon the private sector for its transportation requirements. Such an estimate is not possible, however, for a number of reasons, and in any case it would undoubtedly be challenged as too high (by DOD) and too low (by industry). Rather, the logic of the arguments made is the best basis for a private enterprise solution to defense transportation needs.

---

[20] An entirely new agency, office, or command might be needed to give the concept any chance of succeeding. The scars and bruises within DOD from past "battles" would then heal more quickly. The shipping industry, in particular, would welcome a fresh start.

[21] A collateral question is, Can efficiencies be achieved in commercial as well as defense transportation by combining the present independent regulatory agencies?

EPILOGUE

The year 1976 witnessed several notable transportation events—events that had a direct impact on the ability of U.S. private transportation to meet Department of Defense requirements. On the plus side, a long-sought and necessary railroad deregulation and assistance bill became law—the Railroad Revitalization and Regulation Reform Act of 1976. Industry officials are cautiously optimistic that this new government approach to railroading and its problems will help provide the capital necessary to ensure an upgraded and modern rail system. And on April 1, 1976, the Consolidated Rail Corporation (CONRAIL), successor operator to seven bankrupt northeast railroads, began operations. Reports on its first-quarter operations are encouraging. Thus, with respect to rail operations in the continental United States, defense planners can breathe somewhat more easily.

The trucking industry in 1976 recovered quite rapidly from the effects of the 1974–75 recession. Its plant and equipment are in good shape, and the industry is in general financial good health. And if deregulation proposals become law, trucking should become more efficient economically.

In regard to air transportation, the short-term outlook is for a slow but continuing recovery from the effects of the recession. Deregulation proposals—particularly deregulation of air fares—could be expected to generate increased revenues if enacted. In the long term, however, the picture is not encouraging and should be a major concern of DOD. In a recently released report by the Air Transport Association, it was pointed out that the present rate of return on airline investment *will not* be sufficient to finance the equipment required for anticipated growth and for replacement of aging planes.[1]

---

[1] Air Transport Association, *The Sixty Billion Dollar Question* (Washington, D.C.: Air Transport Association, 1976), p. 7.

161

In this latter respect, new technology to increase fuel efficiency on replacement aircraft is vitally important. The cost, however, is high. The analysis further points out that the present rate of return of between 5 and 6 percent must double by 1980 if the necessary capital is to be internally generated. The report estimates that $65 billion will be needed between 1976 and 1989.

In the past, Department of Defense officials, while very much concerned with the financial health of the airlines, have not participated significantly in Civil Aeronautics Board hearings dealing with questions which affect airline revenues. Nor have DOD officials taken any public position with respect to proposed legislation that directly affects carrier revenues and hence their ability to maintain a modern fleet of aircraft. This reluctance is understandable on the part of an agency that probably feels it already has far too many legislative and bureaucratic battles to fight. Nevertheless, DOD has too much at stake to remain on the sidelines. At a minimum a DOD-CAB liaison should be established on a permanent basis. A viable CRAF depends upon a financially healthy airline industry. Defense input in this respect is essential.

A final event in 1976 is that the Russian military buildup is now perceived as a real threat to NATO. The less than usual congressional cuts in the FY 1977 defense budget are solid evidence of this reality. Although the threat is perceived in the United States, it is surfacing somewhat more slowly in Europe. This situation can be expected to change as more data on Soviet military preparations become available and the threat is understood by the European man in the street.

Now is the time to ask more of our NATO allies, not only in terms of a greater military contribution but also in terms of a full commitment of their commercial transportation assets to the common logistics effort. It was previously stated that the terms under which NATO would contribute merchant ships to a U.S. deployment to Europe should be reassessed. By the same line of reasoning, a meaningful agreement for utilizing NATO's commercial airlift resources should now be pressed. DOD officials and ranking military planners favor the concept and will work for such an agreement. Congressional support, however, is essential if their efforts are to bear fruit. Essentially, the concept of fully utilizing the commercial transportation assets of our allies is but a logical extension of the central thesis of this study.

APPENDIX
The Military Sealift Command Controlled Fleet

Normal (Peacetime) Operations

(1) MSC-owned vessels (nucleus fleet).

(2) MSC equitably owned vessels (build and charter program).

(3) MSC commercially chartered, privately owned ships (voyage and time charter).

Nonmobilization Contingencies

All shipping sources for normal operations and the following:

(1) Vessels from the National Defense Reserve Fleet (NDRF) operated for MSC under General Agency Agreements.

(2) Privately owned ships called up under the Sealift Readiness Program.

(3) Charter of foreign-flag shipping if U.S.-flag ships not available. (During the Vietnam War a total of seventeen foreign-flag ships were chartered by DOD.)

Mobilization

All shipping sources for normal operations and nonmobilization contingencies and the following:

(1) American-flag shipping not under the Sealift Readiness Program.

(2) NATO shipping (by agreement with NATO Planning Board).

(3) U.S.-owned foreign-flag shipping. Note that the value of this shipping in either a contingency or a mobilization is highly questionable. Testifying before the Merchant Marine Subcommittee of the

House Committee on Merchant Marine and Fisheries, Acting Assistant Secretary of Defense John J. Bennett stated: "The Effective U.S. Controlled Fleet (EUSC) should not be considered a substitute for U.S.-flag shipping to accommodate defense needs." In its report to the House of Representatives on the Energy Transportation Security Act of 1974, this subcommittee concluded:

> With respect to the proposed alternative to the HR 8193, i.e., use of the so-called "effective U.S. control" fleet, your Committee carefully evaluated it and found it wanting. Indeed, your Committee finds that the present reliance on it was never intended and that over-reliance on the concept is extremely dangerous and generally inimical to the economic, commercial and national security interests of the United States.

BIBLIOGRAPHY

Aber, J. W. and Gurber, Paul W. "The Navy and Merchant Marine: A Critical Coalition." *U.S. Naval Institute Proceedings*, March 1970, pp. 40–44.

Adams, Brock. "The Shameful State of Transport." *Reader's Digest*, February 1975, pp. 1–6.

Balducci, Ezio. "The Sad Misunderstanding of Section 22." *Translog: The Journal of the Military Traffic Management Command*, November–December 1974.

Besson, Frank S., Jr. "CONEX: Logistics Wonder-Worker in Vietnam." *National Defense Transportation Journal*, June 1966, pp. 34–40.

Blue Ribbon Defense Panel. *Report to the President and the Secretary of Defense on the Department of Defense.* Washington, D.C.: U.S. Government Printing Office, 1970.

Boudreaux, Lionel A. and Cooper, Thomas J. "A Comparative Analysis of the Relationship of Total Distribution Costs Between Airlift and Sealift." Unpublished Master's thesis, Air Force Institute of Technology, 1974.

Budget of the United States Fiscal Year 1976. Washington, D.C.: U.S. Government Printing Office, 1975.

Budget of the United States Government (Annex) Fiscal Year 1975. Washington, D.C.: U.S. Government Printing Office, 1974.

Carlton, Paul K. "Military Airlift Commander Calls For Dynamics Development of All Cargo Aircraft." *Defense Transportation Journal*, December 1975, pp. 26–34.

Case, Frank B. "The Versatile, Vulnerable Containership." *U.S. Naval Institute Proceedings*, February 1972, pp. 48–53.

———. "Time to Secure the Seas." *U.S. Naval Institute Proceedings*, August 1973, pp. 24–31.

Commission on Organization of the Executive Branch of Government.

Transportation: A Report to the Congress. Washington, D.C.: U.S. Government Printing Office, 1955.

Comptroller General of the United States. *Airlift Operations of the Military Airlift Command During the 1973 Middle East War.* Washington, D.C.: U.S. General Accounting Office, 1975.

―――. *Build and Charter Program for Nine Tanker Ships.* Washington, D.C.: U.S. General Accounting Office, 1973.

―――. *Comments on the Department of Defense Report "The Economics of Defense Spending—A Look at the Realities."* Washington, D.C.: U.S. General Accounting Office, 1972.

―――. *Industrial Management Review of the Puget Sound Naval Shipyard.* Washington, D.C.: U.S. General Accounting Office, 1974.

―――. *Status of Selected Major Weapons Systems.* Washington, D.C.: U.S. General Accounting Office, 1975.

―――. *Letter Report B-133025.* Washington, D.C.: U.S. General Accounting Office, 1973.

―――. *Letter Report B-182033.* Washington, D.C.: U.S. General Accounting Office, 1974.

―――. *Letter Report B-181714.* Washington, D.C.: U.S. General Accounting Office, 1974.

―――. *Letter Report B-177692.* Washington, D.C.: U.S. General Accounting Office, 1974.

―――. *Letter Report B-177692.* Washington, D.C.: U.S. General Accounting Office, 1975.

Del Mar, H. R. "Streamlining for Tomorrow." *Defense Management Journal,* April 1975, pp. 32–33.

Durgin, C. T. "Labor-Management Policy and the Maritime College Graduate." *Proceedings of the American Merchant Marine Conference,* December 1954, p. 68.

Elliott, Benton H. and Noble, Philip S. "Intermodal Transportation Systems." *Proceedings Intersociety Conference on Transportation.* New York: Society of Automotive Engineers, 1972.

Expansion of the MSTS Nucleus Fleet: Its Impact on the U.S. Merchant Marine. New York: Harbridge House, Inc., 1969.

Gaddis, W. D. "Logistics and the Future of Navy Transportation." *Defense Management Journal,* April 1975, pp. 23–26.

―――. "Transportation Support for the Navy." *Translog: The Journal of Military Transportation Management,* October 1974, pp. 2–5.

Gorter, Wytze. *United States Shipping Policy.* New York: Harper and Brothers, 1956.

Greenville (S.C.) *News.* July 3, 1975.

Harman, George M. *Transportation: The Nation's Lifelines.* Washington, D.C.: Industrial College of the Armed Forces, 1968.

Hayler, William B. "Our Imperiled State Maritime Academies." *U.S. Naval Institute Proceedings,* June 1972, pp. 50–57.

Huston, James A. *The Sinews of War: Army Logistics 1775–1953.* Washington, D.C.: U.S. Government Printing Office, 1966.

Ignatius, Paul R. "Let the Airlines Play an Optimum Role in Supporting National Defense." *Defense Management Journal,* April 1975, pp. 11–14.

Jollif, J. V. and Kerr, G. D. "Designing for Change: Present and Future." *U.S. Naval Institute Proceedings,* July 1974, pp. 30–38.

Knight, Clayton. *Lifeline in the Sky: The Story of the U.S. Military Air Transport Service.* New York: William Morrow & Company, 1975.

Kornet, Fred, Jr. "Strategic Mobility: The Army Perspective." *Defense Management Journal,* April 1975, pp. 15–19.

Lawrence, Samuel A. *U.S. Merchant Shipping Policies and Politics.* Washington, D.C.: Brookings Institution, 1966.

Locetta, Joseph. "Manpower and the Merchant Marine." *U.S. Naval Institute Proceedings,* July 1970, pp. 26–30.

Locklin, D. Philip. *Economics of Transportation.* Homewood, Ill.: Richard D. Irwin, 1972.

Maclay, Edgar S. *A History of American Privateers.* Freeport, N.Y.: Books for Libraries Press, 1899.

Mahan, Alfred T. *The Influence of Seapower Upon History; 1660–1783.* Louis M. Thacker, American Century Series. New York: Sagamore Press, 1957.

Maloney, Mark L. "Container Crisis." *Army Logistician,* January–February 1975.

McDowell, Carl E. and Gibbs, Helen M. *Ocean Transportation.* New York: McGraw-Hill Book Company, 1954.

Mitchell, Donald W. *History of the Modern American Navy.* New York: Alfred A. Knopf, 1946.

Moore, John E., ed. *Jane's Fighting Ships 1974–75.* New York: Franklin Watts, 1974.

Morris, J. J. "Containers: Their Role in Military Distribution." *Defense Management Journal,* June 1975, pp. 12–18.

Moore, Sam H. "Learning How to Manage Sealift Capability." *Defense Management Journal,* April 1975, pp. 27–31.

National Research Council. *Containership Underway Replenishment: A Study of the Use of Containerships for the Underway Replenishment of Naval Vessels.* Washington, D.C.: National Academy of Sciences, 1971.

————. *Research and Education for Maritime Progress*. Washington, D.C.: National Academy of Sciences, 1973.

————. *The Sealift Readiness Program*. Washington, D.C.: National Academy of Sciences, 1975.

Nevins, Allan. *War for the Union*. 4 Vols. New York: Charles Scribner's Sons, 1971.

New York Times. June 13, 1975.

Official Railway Equipment Register. New York: National Railway Publication Co., April 1975.

Palmieri, John J. "Commercial Shipbuilders: Risk and Reward." *U.S. Naval Institute Proceedings*, August 1975, pp. 46–55.

Patch, Paul F. "Air Enhancement." *Translog: The Journal of Military Transportation Management*, June 1974, pp. 2–5, 14.

Peltier, Eugene J. *The Bureau of Yards and Docks of the Navy and the Civil Engineer Corps*. New York: The Newcomen Society in North America, 1961.

Polmar, Norman. *Soviet Naval Power: Challenge for the 1970s*. New York: Crane, Russak & Company, 1973.

"Portable Scanner Sees Shipments." *Army Logistician*, May–June 1975, p. 39.

Potter, E. B. *The Naval Academy Illustrated History of the U.S. Navy*. New York: T. Y. Crowell Press, 1971.

Riley, Paul H. "DOD Transportation: Management Problems and the Search for Solutions." *Defense Management Journal*, April 1975, pp. 2–5.

————. "DOD Transportation Management Problems and the Search for Solutions." *Defense Transportation Journal*, December 1975, pp. 6–14.

Shott, John G. *Progress in Piggyback and Containerization*. Washington, D.C.: Public Affairs Institute, 1961.

Southern Railway Company. *Stockholder's Newsletter*. March 1975.

"Supertanker Steel Squeeze." *Business Week*, May 18, 1974, pp. 28–29.

Tiedemann, H. J. "Training of Merchant Marine Officers and Seamen." *Proceedings of the American Merchant Marine Conference*, October 1952, pp. 247–249.

U.S. Congress. *Merchant Marine Act of 1920*. Public Law No. 261, 66th Cong., 1920.

————. *Merchant Marine Act of 1936*. Public Law No. 835, 74th Cong., 1936.

————. *Merchant Marine Act of 1970*. Public Law No. 91-469, 92d Cong., 1970.

————. *Merchant Ship Sales Act of 1946.* Public Law No. 321, 79th Cong., 1946.

————. *Shipping Act of 1916.* Public Law No. 260, 64th Cong., 1917.

U. S. Congress, House of Representatives. *Maritime Authorization FY 1976.* 94th Cong., 1st sess., 1975.

U.S. Congress, House of Representatives, Committee on Government Operations. *House Report No. 2011. Military Air Transportation.* 85th Cong., 2d sess., 1958.

U.S. Congress, House of Representatives, Subcommittee of the Committee on Government Operations. *Hearings Military Air Transportation.* 87th Cong., 1st sess., 1961.

————. *Hearings Military Air Transportation.* 88th Cong., 1st sess., 1963.

U.S. Congress, House of Representatives, Subcommittee of the Committee on Armed Services. *Hearings, Proposed Transfer of Military Sealift Command Functions to Military Traffic Management and Terminal Service.* 92d Cong., 1st sess., 1971.

U.S. Congress, House of Representatives, Special Subcommittee on Transportation of Committee on Armed Services. *Report on Proposed Transfer of Military Sealift Command Functions to Military Traffic Management and Terminal Service.* 92d Cong., 1st sess., 1971.

U.S. Congress, House of Representatives, Subcommittee of the Committee on Merchant Marine and Fisheries. *Hearings; Cargo for American Ships, Part 7.* 92d Cong., 1st sess., 1971.

U.S. Congress, House of Representatives, Seapower Subcommittee of the Committee on Armed Services. *Hearings on Current Status of Shipyards 1974.* 3 Parts. 93d Cong., 2d sess., 1974.

U.S. Congress, House of Representatives, Subcommittee of Committee on Appropriations. *Department of Defense Appropriations for 1974, Part 10.* 93d Cong., 1st sess., 1973.

————. *Hearings on Department of Defense Appropriations for 1975.* 93d Cong., 2d sess., 1974.

————. *Hearings on Department of Defense Appropriations for 1976, Part 6.* 94th Cong., 1st sess., 1975.

U.S. Congress, Senate, Committee on Appropriations. *Hearings Department of Defense Appropriations FY 1974, Part 3.* 93d Cong., 1st sess., 1973.

————. *Hearings Department of Defense Appropriations FY 1975, Part 3.* 93d Cong., 2d sess., 1974.

U.S. Congress, Senate, Committee on Commerce. *Report: Transportation of Government Traffic by Civil Air Carriers.* 92d Cong., 1st sess., 1971.

U.S. Congress, Senate, Subcommittee of the Committee on Interstate and Foreign Commerce. *Hearings, Merchant Marine Study and Investigation Transportation of Cargoes by the Military.* 81st Cong., 2d sess., 1950.

U.S. Department of Commerce. *Analyses of Requirement for a Cargo Allocation System.* Washington, D.C.: Maritime Administration, 1973.

————. *Annual Report of the Maritime Administration FY 1965.* Washington, D.C.: U.S. Government Printing Office, 1966.

————. *Annual Report of the Maritime Administration FY 1968.* Washington, D.C.: U.S. Government Printing Office, 1969.

————. *Annual Report of the Maritime Administration FY 1972.* Washington, D.C.: U.S. Government Printing Office, 1973.

————. *Annual Report of the Maritime Administration for FY 1974.* Washington, D.C.: U.S. Government Printing Office, 1975.

————. *Deck and Engine Officers in the U.S. Merchant Marine: Supply and Demand 1974–84.* Washington, D.C.: Maritime Administration, 1974.

U.S. Department of Defense. *Airlift Service Management Report, July 72/ June 73.* Washington, D.C.: Military Airlift Command, 1973.

————. *Annual Defense Department Report FY 1975.* Washington, D.C.: Department of Defense, 1974.

————. *Annual Defense Department Report FY 1976.* Washington, D.C.: Department of Defense, 1975.

————. *The Economics of Defense Spending—A Look at the Realities.* Washington, D.C.: U.S. Government Printing Office, 1972.

————. *Sealift Procurement and National Security (SPANS).* 4 Parts. Washington, D.C.: Department of Defense, 1972.

————. *Ship Register: July, 1975.* Washington, D.C.: Military Sealift Command, 1975.

U.S. Statutes at Large. Vol. 24.

Velie, Lester. "Our Leaky Pipeline to Vietnam." *Reader's Digest,* December 1966, pp. 113–118.

————. "They're Finding Better Ways than Strikes." *Reader's Digest,* March 1974, pp. 42–47.

Walsh, Edmund A. *Ships and the National Safety: The Role of the Merchant Marine in a Balanced Economy.* Washington, D.C.: Georgetown University Press, 1934.

Washington Star-News. January 15, 1975.

Weidenbaum, Murray L. *The Economics of Peacetime Defense.* New York: Praeger, 1972.

Weschler, Thomas R. "Decade of Logistics." *Army Logistician,* January–February 1975, pp. 2–5.

White, Eston T. *Transportation.* Washington, D.C.: Industrial College of the Armed Forces, 1974.

Whitehurst, Clinton H., Jr. "The Merchant Marine Act of 1936: An Operational Subsidy in Retrospect." *Journal of Law and Economics,* October 1965, pp. 223–230.

Yearbook of Railroad Facts: 1975. Washington, D.C.: Association of American Railroads, 1975.

Editor's Note: Several articles and reports treating one or more topics discussed in this study have been published in 1976:

Chase, John D. "U.S. Merchant Marine—For Commerce and Defense." *U.S. Naval Institute Proceedings,* May 1976, pp. 130–145.

Comptroller General of the United States. *Navy Should Reconsider Planned Acquisition of Two Multi-Mission Ships.* Washington, D.C.: U.S. General Accounting Office, 1976.

————. *Letter Report B-181714.* Washington, D.C.: U.S. General Accounting Office, 1976.

Daly, Russel T. "Bringing Air Freight Into the Intermodal Age." *Defense Transportation Journal,* June 1976, pp. 18–26.

Hessman, James D. "A Bluewater Interface and the Running Mates Program: Navy/Merchant Marine Officer Exchange Program Offers Benefits to Each." *Seapower,* June 1976, pp. 20–22.

Hyman, Paul J. "U.S. Defense Transportation Goals." *Defense Transportation Journal,* June 1976, pp. 6–16.

Miller, George H. "The New Soviet Maritime Strategy and the Lack of an Effective U.S. Counter-Strategy." *Seapower,* May 1976, pp. 17–20.

Perlman, Alfred E. "The Role of Intermodality." *Defense Transportation Journal,* February 1976, pp. 6–11.

Polmar, Norman, "A Fleet For the Future: Some Modest Suggestions." *Seapower,* April 1976, pp. 12–17.

Transportation Institute. *Analysis of the Direct Impact of the Merchant Marine on National Security.* Washington, D.C.: 1976.

Zumwalt, Elmo R. "U.S. Seapower: Its Importance in This Age of Technological Change and the Relationship to the U.S. Merchant Fleet." *Defense Transportation Journal,* June 1976, pp. 34–36.